973.7 Schutzer, A. I.
SCH

Great Civil War
escapes

JAN 4	DATE		
	504		
JAN 5 '78	206		
OCT 7	1061		

Great Civil War Escapes

The bloodiest war ever fought on American soil was marked by some of the most daring escapes ever undertaken by prisoners in any century. Author A. I. Schutzer has selected three of the boldest—and most heart-breaking—in the Civil War. Could the tenacity of Union Colonel Thomas Rose enable 109 men to make their way out of the notorious Libby Prison in Richmond? Could the dashing Confederate General John Hunt Morgan and his officers prove that the Ohio State Penitentiary was not the escape-proof prison it was claimed to be? And how did Rebel Sergeant Berry Benson ever hope to make his way from the Elmira Prison Camp and across hundreds of miles of enemy territory to his own lines?

GREAT CIVIL WAR ESCAPES

By A. I. Schutzer

Illustrated by Tran Mawicke

G. P. Putnam's Sons   New York

For Cynthia and Leslie

YOU WILL ALSO ENJOY

WHO GOES NEXT? True Stories of Strange Escapes
by Robert Edmond Alter

FIRST COMES COURAGE
by Robert Edmond Alter

Fourth Impression
SBN: GB 399-60207-0

© 1967 by A. I. Schutzer
All Rights Reserved
Published simultaneously in the Dominion of
Canada by Longmans Canada Limited, Toronto
Library of Congress Catalog Card Number:
67-24168
Printed in the United States of America
12up

Contents

ACKNOWLEDGMENT

I would like to express my gratitude to Jack Hoffman, Robert Connor, Lawrence Sanders, Stuart James, Don McKinney, Clyde Newstrand, Charles Barnard, Harold Straubing, Paul Epstein, Noah Sarlat, Dan Merrin, and especially Thomas MacPherson. Also, I wish to express thanks to Mrs. Ruth Garomon of the Tenafly Public Library and her kind and capable staff, and to the staff of the American History Room of the New York Public Library.

An earlier version of a section of Part Two appeared in True magazine under the title "Breakout!" Gratitude is expressed to the editors of that magazine for permission to use that material in rewritten form here. Copyright 1959 Fawcett Publications Inc.

A.I.S.

Part One
Out of the Rat Hell

I

At daybreak on February 10, 1864, a Confederate sentry did an about-face at the end of his post in an empty lot outside Libby Prison in Richmond, Virginia. When he scanned the east wall of the prison he made out its barred windows and bricks for the first time after a long night. What he saw made his heart pound with alarm.

Jammed inside the prison were more than 1,200 prisoners of war, all Union officers who had been captured in the field. Their exact number on any given day depended on the fortunes of war and the high death rate they suffered from malnutrition and disease.

What the sentinel saw hanging against that east wall of Libby Prison indicated that some of those Union officers had done the impossible—gone through a third-story iron-barred window and crept down the vertical wall like human flies. And they had done this without alerting two Rebel sentries who were close enough to the wall throughout the night to touch it with their fingertips.

"Sergeant of the guard!" bellowed the startled sentry.

The cry of alarm was picked up and passed along from one sentry to the next. Sgt. George Stansil of the 18th Georgia responded on the double. He raced out of the west ground floor room of Libby Prison, a room that served the Confederate prison detail as a combined headquarters, guard room, and sleeping quarters. The sergeant took the steps down to Canal Street two at a time, buckling on his gun belt as he ran. He double-timed the length of the prison, past the cellar rooms flush with street level, going east on Canal Street until he reached the empty lot where the sentinel, who had sounded the cry of alarm, stood open-mouthed, gazing upward.

Sgt. Stansil looked up, too, at a wooden plank swaying in the breeze that blew off the James River. The plank hung from one end of a crude knotted rope, fashioned out of torn strips of horse blanket. The rope was tied to one of the iron bars of the top floor southeast window.

"They've squeezed out somehow!" Stansil said in amazement.

The sergeant of the guard ran off to shake his commanding officer out of bed. A half-hour later, after another quick inspection of the plank that hung from the barred window, a hastily organized party consisting

Colonel Thomas E. Rose

of Major Thomas P. Turner, Libby Prison's commandant, Sgt. Stansil, Adjutant Latouche, E.W. Ross, a civilian clerk employed at the prison, and a heavy detail of Rebel guards, entered the huge rooms where the Union officers were kept prisoner. "Little Ross," so called because he was only four feet and a few inches tall, carried the register of the names of the Federal officers who were kept captive in the prison.

All the prisoners were herded into a loft at one end of the building. They were then forced to pass single file between two parallel lines of guards and then through a doorway—"through the needle's eye," as the prisoners called it—where "Little Ross" ticked off their names in his book.

Although it was bitterly cold in the unheated barnlike loft whose glass windows had long ago been knocked out, "Little Ross" was sweating furiously by the time he had finished checking his roster.

"It's unbelievable!" Ross gasped. "There are 109 prisoners missing!"

The Confederate prison commandant, Major Turner, turned pale. Those near him thought he was going to faint from shock. Finally he stammered out orders that sent messengers flying through the streets of Richmond to the headquarters of General John H. Winder, the officer in charge of all prisoners-of-war held by the Confederacy.

When he arrived at the prison and heard the bad news confirmed, General Winder's lips set in a thin hard line. Only his eyes, black and hard as agates, darting angrily at his trembling subordinates, revealed his pent-up fury.

General Winder personally led a brick by brick inspection of the prison, inside and out. It revealed nothing. How had 109 prisoners-of-war managed to escape?

There was that tantalizing, mystifying wooden plank, dangling from a short horse-blanket rope from a third-story window barred by iron. And there was the three-story-high wall which no man could possibly descend without breaking his neck. That was all.

The General and his trembling prison commandant ended their tour by staring in stupefaction at that bewildering wall.

"They must have squeezed out between the bars somehow," ventured Major Turner.

General Winder promptly exploded. "You fool!" he shouted. "What do you think they did? Crawled down that wall on their hands and knees?"

Major Turner shook his head numbly.

General Winder's voice was hard and biting. "There is only one explanation. The guards—and I don't know who else—were bribed to let my prisoners out!"

Convinced that his solution of how the prison break had been accomplished was the only answer, General Winder wasted no time. In a whiplash voice that struck terror into the hearts of the men around him, he cracked out orders. All sentries who had been on duty the previous night were placed under immediate military arrest and marched off, now prisoners themselves, to

Castle Thunder, a tobacco warehouse in Richmond that had been converted into a prison. Castle Thunder, with àn ominous sound to its name, had an unsavory reputation. There were whispers in Richmond of the brutality of its officials and the cruel pleasure they took in torturing their prisoners.

At Castle Thunder the unhappy Libby sentries were interrogated and then searched for Union "greenbacks" —the money General Winder believed they had taken as a bribe to let 109 Union Army prisoners-of-war go free.

But no bribe money was found on the sentries, all of whom pleaded innocent of any wrongdoing.

And no bribe money could possibly have been found on them. For they had taken none. They were as bewildered by the escape as their superior officers.

Major Turner—with his theory of the men squeezing out between the bars on the windows—was just as wrong as General Winder. When tests were made, it was found that it was physically impossible for even an abnormally emaciated man to slip out between those bars.

For seven days the South wondered. The mystery of how the escape had been executed baffled all except the prisoners who had fled. It was also cause for fear. If there was a hidden escape route out of Libby, it was possible the remaining 1,100 officer prisoners-of-war might use it to walk out of the prison, too. And those men might free the other 15,000 Union soldiers kept captive in the city. If they did, no one dared guess what horrible revenge the Federals might wreak on the city that had imprisoned, starved, and abused them, before they relented and turned their steps north and started to make their way back to Union lines.

II

Just four months and ten days before the big breakout from Libby Prison—shortly after midnight on September 30, 1863—a prison train pulled into the station at Richmond. A young Confederate officer sprang to the platform and bellowed:

"All riii-utt! Let's git them animals off the train!"

The train suddenly came alive, like a segmented caterpillar that had been teased awake against its will. In each car a dark erect shadow—a train guard—walked down the aisle, slapping with his rifle butt at dark formless shapes in the seats. Cries of "C'mon, c'mon, get up, get up—we're here, we're here" came from each car.

Slowly the forms in the seats took shape as men, stretching their arms and legs, groaning, complaining, protesting, standing and moving into the aisles. They were herded out of the cars and to the station platform at gun point, where they were lined up in a ragged column of fours.

Then the march from the station began. A cold wet wind blew across the city, penetrating to the bone. Some of the men shivered and seemed to shrink within themselves. There was no rhythm to their step; they

17

shuffled along. Some wore bloodied bandages. They were a grim-eyed lot, unshaven, dirty, in torn uniforms, without spirit, beaten. For most of them, the war was over.

There were 250 of them. They were Union officers of the Cumberland Army who had been captured on the bloody, brutal battleground of Chickamauga more than 800 miles away.

Among the 250 prisoners was one who limped badly. In this man a strange fire burned. He was that rarest of human beings, a determined escape fanatic, a man obsessed by the notion of getting away from his captors by any means he could. He would permit no obstacle, no setback, no failure on the way, to turn him aside from his goal—and that goal was freedom. He was Col. Thomas Ellwood Rose of the 77th Pennsylvania Volunteers, a slim, dark-bearded, 33-year old veteran of the fighting in Georgia and Tennessee. Col. Rose had enlisted as a private from the coal-mining country of his home state and risen through the ranks. He had already tried to escape when he had jumped from the moving train at Weldon, North Carolina. He had twisted his foot badly when he landed and had barely managed to make it into a pine grove. There he had been flushed out by a Confederate cavalry detachment and put back on the train for Richmond.

The prison that Colonel Rose and his fellow prisoners were being taken to was known as Libby Prison. It had been built by John Enders of Richmond between the years 1845 and 1852 as a warehouse to store tobacco. It was an ill-fated building, one that had been cursed by death and agony even during its construction—when Enders had been killed by a fall from a ladder.

The western end of the building, after it was completed, had been rented to a Captain Luther Libby, a ship's chandler from Maine, for the purpose of conducting his business there. It was Captain Libby's fate to have his name cursed by the more than 50,000 prisoners who passed through Libby while it was held by the Confederacy. Captain Libby had been turned out of the premises and the building commandeered as a prison by General Winder when Richmond had been flooded with captured Union soldiers after the Battle of Bull Run. The captain was not even given time to remove his sign—LIBBY & SON, SHIP CHANDLERS & GROCERS—and there it hung prominently on a corner of the Confederate prison throughout the Civil War. It was a name to be hated, feared, and cursed by the Federal P.O.W.'s who disappeared inside the building.

A half hour after the shuffling column had moved out of the railroad station and started to tramp through the Richmond streets, Libby Prison loomed out of the thick night mist. The huge brick building, some 140 feet long by 110 feet wide, its bottom half white-washed, its windows covered by thick iron bars, seemed to glow in the night.

To Colonel Rose, who was busy etching every detail of his new home in his mind, the building looked like a coffin, with a lighted gas lamp burning at each corner of the box, the sentries surrounding it looking like pallbearers.

As Rose drew abreast of one of the sentinels on Carey Street, he heard the man snicker. "Fresh fish!" the guard called out derisively.

At the corner of Carey and 20th Street the column turned left and started down the hill on which Libby was built. At the intersection of the two streets, tents were pitched. There a Confederate mounted battery was in bivouac, ready to swing into immediate action at any sign of insurrection among the Union prisoners.

On Colonel Rose's left, as he limped down the hill, was the ground or cellar floor of the Libby building. Since the building was built on the side of a hill, its cellar floor was underground at the top of the hill and completely above ground at the bottom where Canal Street ran at right angles to 20th Street.

On Canal Street the column of Union prisoners was turned left again, and then halted in front of the foot of the building. One by one the prisoners were marched up an iron staircase and into the southwest first floor room which served the Confederates as a combined administration, guard, and sleeping room. Each man's name, his rank, and his regiment, were entered in the prison register by the little civilian clerk the prisoners would come to know as "Little Ross." After each prisoner was rostered, his pockets were picked clean by Sgt. George Stansil of the 18th Georgia. Everything of possible value was taken from them: watches, money, pipes, tobacco, rings, spectacles, penknives, even keys —for these could be melted into rebel bullets.

After being stripped of their possessions, the men were pushed into the next room, a large almost bare box, a brick-walled room that measured 44 by 105 feet. Though the prisoners did not know it then, this was the room where they would cook their rations. On the uphill side of the room was a large door which was heavily bolted and guarded on the outside. To the left of this door were several water faucets and an open trough underneath them. The faucets and the trough leaked; the constant overspill on the floor made the room unfit for sleeping. Consequently it usually was deserted at night. There were two or three long pine tables and benches where the men could sit if they chose to eat there. Also there were two cooking stoves. One was ten feet to the right of the Carey Street door. Behind each stove was a fireplace in the brick wall. And behind the brick wall that contained the fireplaces was another room, which the prisoners did not see at this time. It was the same in size as that they were in, bare except for a number of cots, never empty, and it had a small wooden enclosure for a doctor. This room served as the prison hospital.

Col. Rose was sitting on one of the benches in the kitchen room, his head nodding, half asleep, when the last of his group was processed and all were ordered on their feet. He fell in with the others and was led up a staircase in the west end of the huge room.

Rose went up two flights and then was shoved into a big loftlike room. The smell of many men packed together in a closed-in area was sickening. Rose gasped and leaned against a wall.

21

When his nausea subsided, he opened his eyes and looked around. Three or four candles, stuck on the top of condensed milk cans, were burning in various spots around the room, throwing off a feeble wavering light. Several prisoners were gathered in a circle around one of the bigger, brighter candles. From their insignia Rose recognized them as lieutenants, captains, and even a general. All had their trousers off and they were meticulously picking lice out of the seams. As Rose would soon learn, lice-picking was a full-time occupation at Libby.

It seemed that every available inch of the floor was covered by sleeping men. They lay in rows, head to head, and foot to foot. In each row, because there was so little room, the men were sleeping on their sides, packed tightly together in "spoon fashion"—all facing in the same direction, with each man's chest, waist, and bent legs, nested into the man in front of him. None was able to turn over by himself alone; he would break the "nest" if he did. As Rose watched, the man at the head of one row, the row leader, sat up, blew a whistle, and cried out: "Row seven, roll over!" Every man in the row, most of them mumbling and cursing in their sleep, rolled over and faced in the other direction. It was the only way they could turn over during the night.

The faces of the prisoners were deeply lined. They had a desperate, emaciated expression compounded of fear, desperation, and near-starvation. All were under a slow sentence of death. The ration each man drew each day was not enough to keep him alive over an extended period of time. It was not done deliberately by the Confederates, who had hardly enough food to keep their own troops fed adequately, much less any to spare for prisoners. Each prisoner's daily meal consisted of no more than a thumb-sized piece of bread made from ground corncobs; a tablespoon to a cupful of either rice or beans, depending on what was available; and two ounces to a half-pound of bacon which, more often than not, crawled with fat, sluggish-moving, whitish-colored maggots that had to be picked out one at a time.

If this diet did not finish a man off, there was always the possibility of a quick death. The guards were under strict orders to shoot at any prisoners who lingered at the windows, and they were trigger happy. One of the prisoners, a Lt. Hammond, paused a second too long at a window and took a bullet through his ear. Another officer caught a faceful of lead splinters when a minie ball smashed into one of the iron bars across the window a few inches from his head. And an officer of an Ohio regiment was killed when a stray bullet, passing through the window of the floor below his room, continued on through the ceiling and caught him in the head while he read a newspaper ten feet from the nearest window.

III

A few days after Colonel Rose arrived at Libby, he began a systematic search for a way to escape from the prison. Like the other prisoners, he was permitted the free run of the two upper floors during the day. He discovered that each floor was divided into three equal-sized barnlike rooms—an east, middle, and west room.

Each room contained about 250 or more prisoners, was 44 by 105 feet in dimension, and was separated from its adjoining room by a very thick brick partition. The Confederates had knocked openings or doorways into these partition walls so that the men in each room had access to the next. The ground floor contained the west room, used by the Confederates as their office, the middle room, used by the prisoners as a kitchen, and the east room or hospital.

Underneath the ground floor the cellar also consisted of three large rooms which did not have access to one another. The west cellar room, under the Confederate office, contained dungeons where prisoners were put in solitary confinement for any infraction of the rules. The middle cellar room was a kind of carpenter's workshop, store room, and catch-all for any Confederate needs. The east cellar room was rarely used. Its floor was covered with about a foot and a half of straw from the packing cases that had been opened there and was infested with wharf rats. It was known to the prisoners and the Rebels as "Rat Hell," a dark, damp, pestilential hellhole the Rebels visited rarely.

Although it meant risking a bullet in the head from one of the trigger happy guards, Rose managed to steal a look out of the windows on the south side of Libby. He felt it was on that side of the prison, the farthest away from the bivouacked Confederate troops, that an escape might be tried more easily.

From those windows Rose could look out over Canal Street. Just beyond it and running parallel was the Kanawha Canal, a narrow, placid, black channel of water. Next came a narrow strip of land, used as a tow-path for barges on the canal. And beyond that, again parallel, was the broad James River itself. Two or three times each day Rose saw workmen go down through a manhole into a sewer which ran under Canal Street. It occurred to him that this sewer must be at least as high as a man and that it must have additional entrances and exits to the east and west of the prison, some directly into the canal where it discharged its sewage. If he could reach that sewer, he would be able to walk away from the prison in perfect concealment, and then emerge some distance away.

From the east windows of the prison, Rose could look past the vacant lot on that side of the prison at small buildings 60 or 70 feet distant. One, belonging to the James River Towing Co., opened on Canal Street. The significance of the vacant lot and this building did not immediately strike Rose. Nor did he then suspect the importance they would later have in his plans.

The north and west sides of the prison and their intersection where the battery of Confederate mounted troops was bivouacked Rose had seen on the night he arrived at Libby. He discounted them as possible escape sites.

The sewer under Canal Street on the south side of the

prison seemed to offer the best chance of an escape. Was it conceivable he might be able to dig a short tunnel from the cellar of the building to the sewer? But where would he have to make his base of operations? Where would he begin his tunnel?

The cellar room at the west end of the building where the solitary confinement dungeons were located was out of the question, for it was under the Confederate guard room. There was no way of reaching it, except to break through the floor of the Confederate guard room. Even if he could get down to that west cellar room without the Rebs knowing about it, they would hear him digging when he began his tunnel.

Under the hospital room was "Rat Hell." Although prisoners had access to the hospital room by means of sick call, there was no way of getting down to "Rat Hell" undetected. For there were always Confederates present in the hospital room.

That left the room in the middle—the first floor kitchen. It appeared to be the only way Rose might reach the cellar. At one time, because of the overcrowding, prisoners had been permitted to remain in the kitchen at night and sleep on its floor. Now, however, with the faucets and trough leaking, the prisoners avoided the kitchen at night. It was usually deserted—ideal conditions for Rose to search for a way into the cellar.

A few nights after Rose had completed his inspection of the prison, he went down to the kitchen and found it empty. A thin film of water covered the floor. He could hear one of the guards outside, walking his post on Carey Street. Inside, the only sound was the *plink* of the dripping faucets. The room was dark, except for a few chinks of light under the Carey Street door, and the door to the Confederate headquarters room.

Quietly and carefully, Rose walked back and forth across the room, testing the floor. Near the center of the room he found one floorboard that creaked. It was badly warped, and one end had come unsprung. Rose went down on his hands and knees and found he could pry it up with his fingernails, even raise it high enough to make an opening through which a man could pass into the cellar below.

Peering down through the hole, he could not make out anything in the darkness. He had to go down there. Yet how could he get back up?

Finally his gaze settled on one of the long plank benches the prisoners used when they ate in the kitchen. Then he knew he had the makings of a ladder.

He carried the bench to the hole he had made in the kitchen floor. Pushing it through the hole until it touched the cellar floor, he had a ramp running at an angle of about 45 degrees. Rose mounted the bench stomach down, then backed down into the cellar, holding on to the edges to keep from falling.

At the bottom of his impromptu ladder he stood on the cellar floor and waited for a few moments until his eyes adjusted to the darkness. Gradually he was able to start picking out details. To the south was the wall of the cellar that faced on Canal Street. There were two big wooden doors in that wall, and they appeared to be loosely bolted. For a moment, Col. Rose had the wild notion that all he had to do was walk to those doors, unbolt them, and then walk out of the prison a free man.

Then a rude shock brought him back to reality. He heard the measured steps of a sentry, approaching from the east, as he made his rounds along the Canal Street side of the prison. The steps grew louder as the sentry approached the two big doors, and Rose shrank back into the darkness, hiding behind the bench-ramp down which he had descended.

The sentry came abreast of the wooden doors. As he passed the crack between the two big doors, Rose saw his silhouette in the light cast by a street lamp.

"I should have known," he said to himself, "that it could not be so easy . . . that I would not be able to just walk out of the prison. . . ."

Rose waited until the sentry was out of sight, then began a cautious inspection of the cellar room in the murky darkness. East and west the walls were of solid brick; there was no opening to either the cellar room under the hospital room, known as "Rat Hell," or to the dungeons in the room under the Confederate headquarters room.

Rose decided the wall between himself and "Rat Hell" should have a closer inspection. If he could make an opening in that wall, and pass through it, he might be able to start a tunnel in complete secrecy from one of the corners of "Rat Hell."

He felt his way around the celler, looking for some kind of tool, some sharp instrument he could use to

28

test the cellar wall. As luck would have it, he bumped into a work table in the southeast corner of the room. There was a tool box on the table, and a hammer and saw lying next to it. There was a smell of freshly sawn wood, and Rose realized this corner of the cellar must be used as a carpenter's shop of some kind.

He felt around in the tool box until his hand closed on a sharp chisel. Then he made his way back to the wall and began scratching at the mortar between the bricks. It was rock-hard, and Rose made no progress with the chisel. He moved along the wall and tried again, searching for a soft spot where the mortar might have crumbled, and then he heard a noise behind him. He froze where he was for a moment, afraid to move. Some one was at the door, working the bolt handle from the outside. Rose's gaze shot to the kitchen bench that hung down from the ceiling to the floor. If it were seen, he was lost. He would be discovered and thrown into one of the solitary confinement dungeons. And that would be the end of his dream of escape.

If he could move fast enough, however, there was still a chance. Dashing across the cellar, he got his arms around the bench and wrenched it free. Dragging it into a dark corner, he propped it against the wall and huddled in its shadow.

One of the doors on Canal Street creaked partly open. A sentry held the door and let a workman slip past him into the cellar room.

"Hurry," he said. "I'll be in trouble if the sergeant checks the guard now."

"It's only my tools," the workman said. "I was

working in the office upstairs, fixing a drawer for the lieutenant, and I didn't have a chance to come back for my tool box. I don't like to leave it here overnight."

The carpenter made his way across the room to the work table, put his saw and hammer in his tool box, and then, picking the box up, started back for the open door. In a few seconds. Rose heard the big door swinging shut and the bolt dropping home. He was alone in the darkness of the cellar again, and he could hear the two men walking off down Canal Street.

Rose was wet with sweat. It had been a close call. But at least he had the chisel. And now he knew it was hopeless to think of digging a tunnel from this cellar room. It was obvious that workmen came and went from the room and that sooner or later they would spot any escape activity. No, he would have to find something else. And it appeared that his last hope was the cellar room at the east end of the prison under the hospital room. He would have to figure out some way of reaching it.

His immediate problem, however, was to get out of the cellar and back into the kitchen without being discovered. Dragging his ladder-bench back to the center of the cellar room and balancing it on end, he worked the upper portion against the ceiling until he found the loose floorboard. Then he began pulling himself up toward the kitchen.

He had almost reached the top when a hand came down through the hole and grabbed him about the wrist. In a few seconds Rose was through the hole and flopping on the floor of the kitchen room.

Rolling away from the hole, he made out a tall, lean, hawk-faced man. Obviously no Confederate, but a prisoner like Rose, the man was pulling the bench up from the cellar. When he got it out, he carefully tamped the plank flooring back into place with the heel of his boot. Then he extended his hand.

"Major A. G. Hamilton," he said, "of the 12th Kentucky."

"Col. Rose, 77th Pennsylvania Volunteers. Thanks for helping me up." They shook hands.

"It was nothing," the Major said. "You anticipated me tonight. I had already made my own plans to go down into the cellar to see what I could find there. When I came down to the kitchen, I found your hole in the floor. I decided to wait rather than risk running into you in the darkness in the cellar."

Rose smiled grimly. "It might have led to complications."

The two studied each other carefully in the faint light. At last Hamilton asked, "Is there any way out of here through the cellar? Did you find anything?"

Rose described what he had found and said he believed Rat Hell offered the only escape route.

Hamilton nodded. "You're right. And there is a way of getting into Rat Hell. I know. I've given it a lot of thought, and I m almost certain I've figured it out. But it will be dangerous. I was hoping there was another way, an easier way, perhaps in the cellar room immediately below us. But what you learned tonight rules that possibility out."

"What do you have in mind?"

"Well, Colonel," Hamilton said, "first I must tell you I'm a house-builder by trade. I know how a house is made, what holds it up, how thick its walls have to be, how its foundation is laid, how its rafter have to be measured and cut. I can see things in a building that your ordinary soldier cannot."

Rose asked, "You've found something in this building that can help us?"

"I'll explain," Hamilton said. "Each floor in this building appears to have three rooms. Actually, what we have here are three separate adjoining buildings, divided from each other by brick partition walls. "Come with me, Colonel."

Hamilton walked across the kitchen to the northeast corner where one of the cooking stoves stood just ten feet from the Cary Street door. Behind the stove was a fireplace built in the brick wall that separated the kitchen from the hospital room. A smoke pipe ran from the stove into the flue of the fireplace.

Hamilton pointed. "The wall there is almost three feet thick. I know. I measured the walls upstairs where the Rebs cut doorway openings. Do you know what that means, Colonel?"

Rose's face lighted up. "Yes! A wall as thick as that could hold a man inside it, and nobody would be the wiser. Fantastic!"

"What I had in mind," Hamilton said, "was to break into the back of the fireplace and then tunnel down inside the wall. We must be very careful to preserve a shell on both sides of the wall so we don't break through the wall on the other side into the hospital room or on this side, below us, into the cellar room. We go down inside the wall far enough to get below the floor of the hospital room. Then we break through the wall on that side—into the cellar—and we're in Rat Hell. Then we can start tunneling from Rat Hell. We would be undisturbed. The Rebs don't like that room. It gets flooded when the canal is high, and it is infested with wharf rats. They stay away from it as much as they can."

Rose said, "We'll have to break into the wall and dig only at night when the kitchen is deserted. And every morning we'll have to close up the hole and cover it up before the other prisoners come down to cook their breakfast."

There was nothing more the two prisoners could do that night. They went up to the lofts, found their allotted few inches of floorspace, and bedded down for the night.

IV

The next night, a little after ten o'clock, the infantry colonel and the cavalry major went down to the deserted kitchen and began to work on the fireplace. They had to work carefully and quietly, for they could hear the sentry pacing back and forth on Carey Street just a few feet away.

Rose swept the soot out of the fireplace on to a rubber poncho he had managed to keep. Every drop of the dirt would be carefully saved—to be thrown back into the fireplace later and smeared over the seams and bricks to conceal the signs of their work.

Rose stood lookout so they would not be taken by surprise. Hamilton, the housebuilder with experience in bricks and mortar, took the broad-bladed chisel Rose had stolen and began to chip away at the seams between the bricks. As each piece of mortar came out, and then the bricks, one after the other, they were placed on the poncho and carefully laid out in position so that each could be put back in the exact spot when the night's digging was finished.

Shortly before four o'clock in the morning, the two quit working. Bricks were put back into place, mortar chips and dust were squeezed back into the seams, and soot smeared over them and thrown back on the fireplace floor. To the casual eye, from a distance of as little as three or four feet away, there was no sign that any digging had taken place.

It took Hamilton, working in a head-down position with his feet held by Rose, 15 nights to dig down through the wall. On that last night he broke through the wall, under the floor of the hospital, into the cellar room known as Rat Hell. In all, between 50 and 75 bricks had been dug out. All were replaced at the end of each night's digging. Every one of the bricks, except for 12 that were put back into the fireplace wall to conceal the hole, would later be hidden under the straw in Rat Hell. When completed, the tunnel inside the wall ran from the kitchen room fireplace down below the floor of the hospital room and then through the wall of the cellar room.

Sixteen nights after they had started, Rose sat in the

fireplace with his legs dangling in the hole. He was going down into the hole in the wall to make the complete trip into Rat Hell for the first time.

As Hamilton watched anxiously, Rose let himself slide into the hole. When his body was all the way in and his head was below the fireplace floor, he held on to the edges of the hole for a few seconds before letting himself drop the rest of the way.

He dropped perhaps six inches to the bottom and started through the bend at the bottom. As his legs got into the bend, he suddenly slipped farther. His chest became wedged in the narrower bottom of the vertical shaft, his arms pinned over his head. He was stuck.

"I can't breathe," he gasped. "Help me, Hamilton!"

Hamilton crept into the fireplace and held a candle down into the shaft. He could see that Rose was stuck solidly in the shaft, his arms wedged over his head.

"Don't move," he whispered. "You'll only get yourself in tighter. I'll grab you by the wrists and pull you back up."

Straddling the hole, Hamilton locked his hands around Rose's wrists and heaved. There was no give at all. Rose was trapped.

"We can't do it," Hamilton grunted. "We'll have to give it up. I'll have to ask the Rebs to help us or you'll die in there."

"No," Rose groaned. "Go upstairs and get one of our own men—somebody you can trust. Hurry!"

Hamilton backed out of the fireplace and ran up to the room where most of the men who had been captured at Chickamauga slept. These men had been taken prisoner with Col. Rose and would recognize his name.

Hamilton stumbled blindly across the room, tripping over the sleeping forms. He was not sure which man to approach. Any one he spoke to would be a gamble.

In one corner of the room young Lieutenant F. F. Bennett of the 18th Regulars who had been unable to fall asleep that night, sat up and gripped Hamilton by the leg as the major stumbled frantically from sleeper to sleeper.

"What's wrong, friend?" Bennett whispered.

Something about the calm assurance of the voice steadied Hamilton. He knelt quickly beside Bennett and studied his face. Instinctively he trusted him—and told him of Rose's predicament.

Bennett nodded and got to his feet. With Hamilton leading, the two stumbled over and stepped on the cursing men on the floor, not caring where they set their feet in their rush to get down to the kitchen.

This time Hamilton took one of Rose's wrists and Bennett took the other. They spread their legs, crounched, and heaved upwards, but Rose's body did not budge. Even more disturbing, there was no sign of life from Rose. His head sagged to one side.

Hamilton and Bennett tried different tactics. They pulled alternately on Rose's arms, sawing him back and forth. Finally the grip the walls of the shaft had on Rose's chest was broken and his body lurched upwards.

They dragged Rose away from the fireplace and laid

37

him out on the floor. He appeared dead at first, but after a few minutes his chest began to rise and fall. Hamilton, seeing that Rose was coming around, went back to the fireplace, bricked up the opening, and covered it with soot from the poncho.

Hamilton and Bennett half-carried Rose up the stairs, laid him out in a corner, and squatted next to him. By this time Rose was able to speak weakly.

"I'm grateful," he whispered to Bennett. "When we're ready, we'll take you on the escape. You can depend on that."

Rose spent the next night recuperating while Hamilton went down to the kitchen alone. He opened the shaft in the fireplace wall and, by knocking out a number of bricks, enlarged the shaft sufficiently so that a man could pass through it without getting stuck.

The next night Rose was ready to go down to the kitchen again with Hamilton. The two opened up the fireplace and Rose entered the tunnel first. This time there was no mishap. He squirmed through the shaft into the Rat Hell cellar room. To make the return to the opening in the wall from the cellar floor of Rat Hell easier, Rose fixed an ingenious ladder. He had made it from a rope given him by Col. Harry White, one of the Union officers in charge of the used clothing sent down from the North to be distributed among the enlisted Federal prisoners held in the nearby Belle Isle Prison. Col. White had stolen the rope, which had tied a bale of clothing. It was about 100 feet long and an inch thick.

A length of rope Rose had left after making his ladder he saved for later use in the tunnel they planned to dig.

Rose and Hamilton inspected the cellar room, lighting their way with a small candle. The air of Rat Hell was damp and chill, the floor covered with packing straw where rats could be heard scurrying about.

Rose led Hamilton to the southeast corner of the room and said, "Just outside here is a manhole in the center of Canal Street. It leads down into a sewer. I know because I've seen city workmen go down to work in the sewer. It must be at least six feet high, maybe a little more, because when the men drop into it the tops of their heads do not reach street level. We can dig a short tunnel from here to that sewer. Once we break into the sewer, we can walk east or west underground to get away from the prison. We can come out either through a manhole opening a mile or two away, or we can go right into the James River Canal into which I'm certain the sewer drains."

Hamilton agreed to Rose's plan. The next night the two came down to Rat Hell, prepared to start their digging. They attacked the floor along the south wall, in its eastern corner, using the chisel Rose had stolen. Since the cellar floor was at ground level at that point, they had to dig straight down to get under the building wall. After they were past the wall, they planned to level out and go straight for the sewer.

Rose dug by candlelight while Hamilton stood lookout and helped in any way he could. From upstairs they had brought a wooden spittoon about eight inches square by five inches deep; they tied lengths of rope to its opposite ends.

They worked in this way: Rose, digging in the tunnel, put the dirt he chiseled into the spittoon. Hamilton, at the mouth of the tunnel, drew the spittoon out by his end of rope when Rose signaled by a tug that it was full. Then Hamilton dumped the dirt under the straw on the floor and Rose pulled the empty spittoon back by his end of rope.

At the end of each night's digging, the two returned to the kitchen upstairs through the shaft in the wall, resealed the fireplace opening, and covered it with the soot they had saved.

All went well at the beginning. But it soon became obvious that the digging of a tunnel from Rat Hell to the sewer was too big a job for two men. Rose would dig in the tunnel for a while, and then his air would go bad. He would start gasping and his candle would flutter out. Hamilton became exhausted quickly too. Neither was up to normal strength; both were suffering from the starvation diet.

They needed help. But whom could they trust? All the prisoners believed that the Confederates frequently sent spies into Libby disguised as Union prisoners in order to ferret out escape schemes. They agreed they could trust Bennett. But they needed more men.

Picking their men carefully, they selected 13, including Bennett, and swore them to secrecy about the plan. Now there were 15 tunnelers, whom Rose divided into three work parties of five men each. Each group worked one night and had the next two nights off in which to rest and recover from the ordeal of digging. Somewhere they turned up pocket knives to aid them.

When the tunnel reached the wall, the diggers hit an unexpected obstruction: the foundations were laid on massive timbers, piled in depth. Some of the men were discouraged. It did not appear they could make a dent in the hard wood with their chisel and knives.

Rose turned the tunnel downwards, planning to pass under the timbers before straightening out again. He took the lead himself. One night as he bored deeper under the timbers, the earth turned soft and moist. It was a danger signal, but Rose, in his preoccupation, did not take notice.

Little by little the bottom of the hole began to fill with water. Soon the earth became soft mud. Suddenly there was a gurgling sound and the wall of earth in front of Rose collapsed completely. Water poured through the gap into the tunnel shaft, taking Rose by surprise. He started to scramble backwards, but was too late. Water filled the tunnel in a matter of seconds, and Rose lost consciousness.

When he came to he was lying on the Rat Hell floor where he had been dragged by the other tunnelers. Hamilton was at his side. They agreed they must have dug below the level of the nearby canal. What should they do now?

"Plug up the hole," Rose said. "We'll have to find another way of getting to the sewer."

For a few nights they stopped digging. And then, early one morning, Rose led Hamilton close to one of the barred windows on the southeast side of the prison. "Look quickly," he said, "so you don't draw fire from the sentries. Straight down there, at the corner of the building, there's a depression in the ground. It runs like a ditch right out to the center of the street. The only thing it can mean is that there's a drain pipe buried underground there—running from the building to the sewer. We can dig into that drain and then crawl along it to the sewer. Then we can break into the sewer and we're out."

The other tunnelers were told of the new plan and digging started again. The drain pipe was reached quickly, but then they found its diameter was too small for a man to crawl through it. The pipe was not a solid unit, however. Its walls consisted of planks butted against each other, side against side. Rose measured one of the planks and found it was three inches thick. As a result, he ordered the men to strip the planks out, leaving a shaft whose diameter was increased by six inches and thus making a passage down which a man could crawl.

The plank-stripping was a tedious, exhausting, muscle-cramping struggle in the overpowering stench of the sewage which drained from Libby Prison. Rose pushed it doggedly. By the night of January 25, 1864, the tunnelers were within one plank-length of the main sewer under Canal Street. Jubilantly the men knew they were only a few feet from freedom.

That night extra precautions were taken. Only two men went into Rat Hell instead of the usual five—to lessen the risk of exposure. Their assignment was to remove the remaining planks that blocked the way, to break into the main sewer, and then to stay in Rat Hell all of the next day to make sure no Rebels found the tunnel opening. At night they were to go up through the fireplace opening and tell the others, who would be waiting in the kitchen.

January 26 was a long and anxious day for the 13 men waiting in the upstairs rooms. They tried to keep themselves busy by getting their belongings together and working out routes for the march to the north, but the hours dragged interminably.

Finally darkness came. The 13 men descended to the kitchen and opened up the fireplace hole. Minutes passed. Then they heard one of the men coming up through the hole in the wall. His head emerged. By the look on his face they knew they had failed again.

"It's hopeless," he said bitterly. "We worked all night and all day and could do nothing. The wood in the main sewer is petrified. It's like rock. We could not even scratch it with the chisel."

The 15 tunnelers had been digging for 39 nights, most of the time in the nauseating stench of the small sewer drain. They had sweated in constant fear of discovery and punishment—possibly hanging. Now, when success had appeared to be within their grasp at last, they had failed again.

One by one the 13 men went to Rose and told him

43

they could not go on. They were quitting. Only one man stuck with Rose-- Major Hamilton.

V

Together Colonel Rose and Major Hamilton started another tunnel.

This time they went to the northeast corner of Rat Hell, just ten feet from the sentry who paced outside on Carey Street, and broke into the east stone wall six inches above floor level. There were stone fenders jutting into the cellar from this wall, about 20 feet apart, and the two dug in the wall space between the end fender and the north wall in almost total darkness.

This new tunnel had one important factor in its favor. Ground level outside this corner of Libby Prison was just above the ceiling of the cellar. It was about 10 feet higher than ground level at the Canal Street side of the prison where they had been digging previously. Thus, they did not have to tunnel downwards to get under the surface of the earth. They could go straight forward and not worry about canal water breaking the walls of their tunnel.

Rose planned now to tunnel 50 or more feet straight across and underneath the vacant lot next to the east wall of the prison. This could carry him under a high wooden fence on the other side of the lot. His goal was to come up on the other side of the fence through the floor of a carriage shed that could be seen from the east windows of the prison. In that shed were stored packages of food and clothing sent to the prisoners from the north. The escapers then could leave this shed and go south concealed from the sentries by the high wooden fence.

This would bring them to a small storage building on Canal Street occupied by the James River Towing Co. At this point they would have to come out in the open on Canal Street and might run into trouble. They would have to leave the towing company building in the glare of a gas lamp and the sight of the sentinels who paced on the Canal Street side of Libby Prison. But Rose believed that if they moved fast and timed themselves carefully they woud be able to leave as the nearest sentry was walking away from them to the end of his beat some 100 feet away. In that interval, the escapers could hurry east along Canal Street into the dark gloom of Richmond at night. Their only fear of being apprehended was a chance brush with one of the roving patrols of the Confederate provost guard in Richmond.

In one night Rose and Hamilton breached the east stone wall with their broad-bladed chisel, digging out the mortar between the stones, and then lifting out the stones themselves. They made a hole, roughly circular in shape, slightly more than two feet in diameter, its bottom just about six inches from the floor.

Once through the wall they hit densely compacted sand. They started to tunnel through this, and when they were about six feet along the way they ran into a familiar problem. The digging was a job beyond the physical resources of two already exhausted—though fanatically determined—men.

There was only one solution, and Rose and Hamilton

45

did not hesitate. They had to enlist a new party of diggers. This they did, even managing to convince some of the old diggers to return to the task. Once again, there were 15 tunnelers. Rose divided them into three work parties of five, to dig 12 out of 36 hours, for they were working around the clock now.

The savage, repetitive, dangerous, and exhausting routine of moling through the earth began once again. Once more their implements were chisel, wooden spittoon box, rope, and tallow candle. The head of the tunnel was narrow, dark, and damp, and the tunnelers began to think of it as a grave.

Absolute caution was essential at all times, for it appeared the Confederate prison authorities had become suspicious that some kind of escape scheme was under way. They had suddenly instituted a new routine. At least once every day a detail of Confederate guards, commanded by a sergeant of the 18th Georgia, made an inspection tour of the prison.

A regular stop on the inspection itinerary was Rat Hell. When the Confederate guard detail marched to a halt on Canal Street, just outside the bolted and locked door, the lookout gave the warning. All work stopped. The digger backed his way to the mouth of the tunnel so that he would not be trapped inside it if they were caught. Straw was thrown over the opening, and the other men hid in the shadows of the stone fenders that jutted out from the wall or burrowed under the packing straw on the floor. The north end of Rat Hell, where the tunnel began, was dark anyway, and the Rebel guards did not care to venture too deeply into the pestilential cellar room with its damp, foul smells and the constant rustle of scurrying wharf rats. A bite from one of those huge rodents meant an inevitable infection, sometimes death. So the inspecting guards usually just poked their heads inside the south door, or perhaps rummaged around in the straw near the door for a few minutes, and then went away.

With a tunneling team of five men digging in the cellar during the daylight hours, Rose was hard pressed to conceal their absence from the count that was taken of the prisoners twice a day, at nine in the morning and four in the afternoon, by E.W. Ross, the civilian clerk.

For the count, the 1,200 prisoners were lined up in four ranks in one of the loft rooms. At each count, Rose maneuvered himself and four of his off-duty men near the head of the line. As soon as they were counted, they slipped out of line and worked their way, bent double, through the other prisoners to the rear ranks where "Little Ross," who had trouble seeing over the heads of the men in the first row, counted them a second time and got what he thought was a correct tally.

One day some of the other prisoners, knowing nothing of the tunnel or the reason why Rose and his men were doubling back and forth to make the count come out right, became convinced that the scurrying back and forth was simple horseplay to have a laugh on the Confederate clerk and guards. When the prisoners fell in for the count, these men lined up with Rose and four of his off-duty tunnelers at the head of the line.

When the diggers started to slip back through the ranks to the end of the line, these men followed them. Broad grins on their faces, they were counted a second time too. Rose and his men were furious. But they dared not say anything for fear of arousing the suspicions of the Confederates. It did them no good, however, to remain silent. The impossible total he got threw the little clerk into a frenzy.

"Dammit," squeaked "Little Ross" as he peered up from his tally sheet, "I got 15 more men in my count than we got prisoners! What's going on here?"

Both guards and prisoners roared with laughter. Ross, fuming impatiently, took another count. This time, somehow, it came out right.

But the seed of suspicion had been planted in the minds of the Confederates. And Rose was aware of it. "We'll have to be careful at the count tomorrow," he told Hamilton. "If we have a repetition of what happened today, the Confederates will know something is wrong."

The next day, only two men were permitted to go down to work on the tunnel during daylight hours and be absent from the count—Major B.B. McDonald and Captain I.N. Johnston.

Rose's fears were well-founded. When the Rebels turned up for the morning count, they brought double the usual number of guards. The count began in its usual fashion with "Little Ross" ticking off heads four at a time. In spite of the tightened security, two of the off-duty tunnelers attempted to slip from the front ranks to the rear in order to cover up for McDonald and Johnston. The other prisoners had had enough of what they thought was horseplay at the Confederates' expense, however. They were afraid that the prisoners would be punished generally if the count came out wrong. They closed ranks on the two diggers, refusing to permit them to pass through to the end of the line. There was some pushing and shoving and the Confederate guards wanted to know what was going on. The Rebel officer in charge of the count warned the prisoners that any offenders would go down to the solitary confinement cells.

The count was completed without further incident, and the clerk's tally revealed that two men were missing. After a hurried consultation between the civilian clerk and the Confederate guards, it was decided to pass the prisoners "through the eye of the needle." Each man's name was called and he was forced to pass through a doorway from one loft room to the next as he was checked off the roll.

This time there was no question about it. Major McDonald and Captain Johnston were missing. And the Confederates now knew that either they had escaped or were in hiding somewhere in the prison.

That night, when the fireplace passage was opened up, Rose gave McDonald and Johnston the bad news. The tunnelers had not been able to cover up for them at the roll call that day. "You can either come up and turn yourself in with some kind of story," he told them, "or stay missing. If you choose the latter, it means you will have to stay down and hide yourself in Rat Hell until we finish the tunnel and you can go out with the rest of us."

McDonald and Johnston looked at each other. "Not for me," McDonald said. "If I have to live 24 hours a day in that dark hole without a break, I'll go mad. I'll take my chances with the Rebels. If they don't believe what I tell them, the worst they can do is throw me into solitary confinement for a couple of days."

"I'll stay down," Johnston said. "The Rebs might believe they missed one man in roll call, but not two. Let them think what they want to about my disappearing. It'll keep them busy."

McDonald returned to the lofts upstairs, while Johnston went back alone to Rat Hell. The moment McDonald was spotted by the other prisoners, he became the center of a curious crowd who wanted to know where he had been at roll call. Word of his mysterious reappearance reached the Confederates and he was hustled down to the headquarters room for an interrogation.

"I fell asleep," McDonald told the Rebels, "under a raincoat in a corner of the upper west room. The guards must have missed me when they rounded up the men for roll call yesterday."

The Rebels accepted McDonald's story and sent him back to the lofts. Where Johnston had disappeared to, they could only wonder about along with everybody else. The final consensus among the other prisoners and the guards was that somehow, in some mysterious manner, he had managed to escape. They did not suspect that each night his companions went down through a hole in the wall in the building to bring him food.

Rose and the others decided to abandon daytime digging as too dangerous. Since Johnston's disappearance, the Rebels had become extremely careful at roll call to see that no mistakes were made and it became impossible to shift around in ranks and beat the count.

Each night, however, a few hours after the sun went down, a party of diggers descended through the fireplace opening in the kitchen to Rat Hell where they were greeted by Johnston. He was starved for human company, and the arrival of the tunnelers was a welcome event.

Night after night the work progressed. The tunnel was pushed deeper and deeper into the lot on the east side of the prison. The men knotted their rope in one-foot lengths and made a rough estimate of their progress by pulling it forward into the tunnel. It *appeared* that they had gone 53 feet into the earth, but there was no way of telling precisely how far they had gone. The problem of solving exactly where the head of the tunnel stood was solved for the diggers in an unexpected manner.

The tunnel had begun to assume a personality of its own, a kind of black maw that swallowed a man and then spit him out hours later, choking and gasping for air. It was an endless cylinder in the wall into which a

51

man crawled on his hands and knees, a narrow black tomb from whose sides clods of earth and sand fell constantly, ground between a man's teeth, lined his eyelids, rubbed deep into his scalp, always carrying the threat of a collapse and sealing a man alive deep inside the earth.

The solitude at the head of the tunnel where only one digger could work at a time began to affect the men. The darkness, the foul air, the cramped quarters, the wavering candle light did strange things to their minds. Fear became something tangible in the sweat that poured from their bodies. Their own minds and their imaginations became their greatest enemy. Each was affected differently by the ordeal. One or two, after hours of chipping away at the earth, became convinced that they were lying in their coffins and already buried deep in the earth. When that happened, panic set in very quickly, and the victim pushed himself backwards out of the tunnel in a rush with a jerky, hysterical, crablike movement. Others found, after chopping away at the earth at the head of the tunnel for an hour or two, that they lost all power to move or take any kind of action whatsoever. They could lie for hours, immobile the chisel lying uselessly in their trembling fingers, staring in stupefaction at the blank earth wall ahead of them. It seemed to shimmer hypnotically in the flickering candlelight.

One night, McDonald, unknown to those behind him in Rat Hell, began digging straight upwards in a fury, convinced that the tunnel had already overshot its mark and that further forward digging was senseless torture.

In ten minutes McDonald literally erupted from the earth. His head stuck out of a hole in the ground in the empty field on the east side of the prison. He was about ten feet short of the fence, and only the fact that it was night prevented the guard pacing on the east side of the prison from seeing him.

McDonald hastily dropped back into the tunnel. Thoroughly cowed now, he scrambled back down the tunnel into Rat Hell and told the other men what he had done. They were stunned. Nobody knew what to do. Finally, Major Hamilton told everybody to stay where they were. Nobody was to go into the tunnel. He would go upstairs and consult with Rose, who was sleeping at the time.

It was about midnight when Hamilton woke Rose and told him about the disaster. The two officers conversed in subdued tones, trying to figure out whether the sentry had seen the hole in the ground. They went to the east windows and surreptitiously looked down at the vacant lot. All seemed quiet down there. They couldn't make out where the hole was. The guard did not seem to have given an alarm yet. If they were lucky, he had seen and heard nothing. But if he had spotted the opening, the Confederates might be lying in wait to trap the first man who came down the tunnel to the opening. There was only one way to find out. Somebody had to take a chance and go into the tunnel.

VI

Rose went into the tunnel and crawled forward alone. When he reached the break he cautiously squeezed his head through it and rested his chin on its edge. Looking around, he tried to assess the damage.

They were about ten feet from the fence, about 15 feet short of their goal, the carriage shed whose floor they hoped to reach. The break McDonald had made was on the eastward slope of a slight depression in the ground and out of the direct line of sight of the sentry when he marched along the wall of the prison. The darkness, too, helped to conceal the hole in the ground.

Feeling better about the situation, Rose dropped back into the tunnel. In the cramped quarters he squirmed out of his shirt, packed it with dirt and sand, and then shoved it upwards to plug the hole. If it held, if nobody stepped on it in the open field and broke through, then they still had a chance. That done, Rose backed down the tunnel shaft to the opening. He ordered the men to dig in a downwards direction for the next two or three feet before going forward again, and then went upstairs and back to sleep.

The next night Rose returned to the tunnel. He reopened the hole McDonald had made, shoved an old shoe out on the ground, and then replugged the hole with his shirt. The vacant lot was littered with an assortment of junk anyway, thrown out of the windows by prisoners, and the shoe would attract no special attention during the day.

When the sun came up the next morning, Rose was at one of the east wall windows, peering through the iron bars. He located the shoe and got an exact idea of just where the tunnel had reached, how far it had to go yet to make it to the shed, and in what direction. He issued the necessary orders to the diggers who were scheduled to go down that night.

All during the latter part of the digging of the tunnel, a detail of Confederate guards had regularly paid its daily inspection visit to Rat Hell, taken a brief look into the south end of the cellar, and then continued on its rounds. Each time Captain Johnston hid in a hole he had made for himself in the straw in the north end of the cellar. He had been able to observe the Rebels without being seen himself.

On Saturday, February 6, 1864, there was unusually heavy Confederate traffic in Rat Hell. The regular inspection team of Confederate guards had been almost doubled. They stayed longer than they usually did and took more than a cursory look. They made their way into the north end of the cellar where Johnston was hiding and kicked at the straw. Several guards stood and talked in low tones within inches of the straw-covered tunnel mouth.

One brought in a dog and the hound went rat-hunting, racing back and forth through the straw. Although the dog almost stepped on Johnston's face once or twice, it ignored him. Then the guards left.

Just as Johnston was about to leave his place of hiding, the Canal Street door was thrown open again and a Confederate sergeant came in with a work party of Negroes. They appeared to be after some empty barrels stored in the back of the cellar. In one of the barrels the men found a haversack of food left behind by one of the digging party. The men divided the food up and ate it.

That night Johnston took Rose aside and told him about the large Confederate inspection party and the careful search. The two discussed the haversack of food the Rebel work party had found and eaten. Would the Rebels figure out that the food could only have been left behind by a prisoner who had no business in the cellar?

Rose spread the word among the other members of the escape party. Their tunnel was almost completed—just a matter of several feet of earth separated them from freedom—and now the Rebs seemed to suspect an escape scheme.

Time was short. The tunnel had to be finished—and quickly—before the Rebels blundered on it, or all their work would be lost.

The next day, Sunday, was the one day in the week when the Rebels did not inspect the prison. That meant, if the Confederates kept their normal schedule, there would be no visitors to Rat Hell. Rose decided to take the risk of tunneling during the daylight hours, but limit the number of tunnelers to as few as possible in order to minimize the risk.

Before daylight on Sunday morning he went down into Rat Hell through the fireplace opening, taking only McDonald with him. Johnston was assigned to lookout duty, and McDonald was given the job of fanning air into the tunnel. Rose went into the tunnel himself to dig. He decided to dispense with the spittoon, figuring he had less than 5 feet to go now and could make better time by spreading the dirt evenly behind him in the tunnel.

All that day Rose chipped away at the earth and sand without a break. When night came, he backed agonizingly out of the tunnel and staggered like a drunken man as he tried to stand. McDonald and Johnston half-carried him to the rope ladder so that he could make his way up through the fireplace opening. But the effort seemed to have been worth it. Before falling into a deep sleep, Rose whispered to Hamilton that he had gone almost twice the distance any previous digging party had gone in one shift.

"I think one more day like this will finish it," Rose said hoarsely, "or finish me."

On Monday morning, before the sun came up, Rose went down into Rat Hell again. It was February 8, 1864. McDonald was with the colonel to fan air into the tunnel, and Johnston, by now the ratty-looking full-time resident of the cellar, was the lookout.

They were on the seventeenth day of work on this tunnel, and Rose was determined to finish the job that day. For over 16 straight hours, without a break, he dug in the foul, suffocating air of the tunnel. An hour or two before midnight he struck the bottom of a wooden post and guessed correctly he was passing under the fence at the east end of the vacant lot.

An hour later he started to dig up. Exhausted, he lay on his back and chopped at the earth above him. Clods of dirt fell down on his face and clogged his nostrils and filled his mouth. More than once he was seized by spasms of uncontrollable retching. His lungs ached with the pain of each breath of fetid air.

Rose felt himself getting weaker. He let the chisel slip from his fingers and pounded at the earth roof over his head with his fists. And then, miraculously, the earthen crust gave way and his balled-up hands broke through the dirt floor of the shed. Rose agonizingly pulled himself up on his feet and sucked great gulps of clean, fresh air deep into his lungs.

"We're through," he sobbed, "we're through. We made it at last."

The fresh air soon restored his strength. Pulling himself the rest of the way out of the hole and brushing himself off, he stepped out of the shed into the yard. The high wooden fence concealed him from the sentries on the east side of the prison, and he was free to move about as he pleased. He walked to the James River Towing Co. building on Canal Street. It had one exit, an arched gate, held closed by a heavy horizontal bar. Rose swung the bar back out of the way, pulled the gate open, poked his head out, and peered down Canal Street at the prison. He saw the guard on the south side of the prison walking away from him. To the east the road was clear and the way lay open into Richmond.

His survey completed, Rose went back to the shed. He found a plank of wood and, when he went back into the tunnel, pulled it over the opening he had made in the floor. Then he crawled back down the tunnel to Rat Hell where he broke the news that the tunnel was completed to McDonald and Johnston.

Rose and McDonald went up to the kitchen through the opening in the fireplace. While McDonald closed up the hole and smeared soot over the bricks, Rose went upstairs. He sought out Major Hamilton, took him aside, and whispered the news.

Rose returned to the kitchen while Hamilton rounded up the other members of the digging party. In a few minutes the men were gathered around Rose in the darkened kitchen. "Boys," he told them, "the tunnel is finished."

It was then about three o'clock in the morning. Rose, Hamilton, and one or two of the men still wanted to go out that night. They feared the tunnel might be discovered during the day and that all their effort might still be lost. But the majority of the tunnelers were willing to sweat out one more day so that when they left they would have a full night in which to work their way out of Richmond.

The majority view prevailed, and Rose and Hamilton agreed to go along with the wishes of the men. Then a question arose: Should they tell any of the other prisoners about the tunnel so that they, too, could try a break?

After a long and bitter discussion, the members of the escape team agreed that each could pick one friend who might become a member of a second escape party.

59

These men would be sworn to wait one full hour after the tunnelers went into the tunnel before they left the kitchen and went down into Rat Hell. This would give the diggers a chance to get away from the immediate area of the prison before any one else left.

Colonel H.C. Hobart of the 21st Wisconsin was asked to cover the tracks of the escapers who left that first night by rebuilding the fireplace wall. He himself would organize still another escape team and take them out on the following night. Before going, he would deputize another officer to cover *his* tracks, form still another escape party, and take them out on the third night. This officer in turn would deputize another officer to lead an escape party on the fourth night, and so on—until the prison was either cleared or the Confederates discovered the tunnel.

"We've really got the fever now," McDonald marveled. "We're forgetting that after the escape there will be a roll call in the morning at nine o'clock. When the Rebs find we're gone, they'll tear the prison apart to find out how we got out."

"Maybe we can throw them off the track," Rose said, "by convincing them we got out by some means other than a tunnel. Through one of the windows, for instance. After dark tomorrow night, we'll leave a rope hanging from the bars of one of the windows. Maybe even tie a plank to it. It'll give them something to think about."

After a day of unnerving tension, the night of February 9, 1864, finally came. It was cold, the sky was clear, and there was a bright moon. By 7 P.M. The Tunnelers had filtered down to the kitchen one by one. At 8 P.M. Rose removed the bricks from the fireplace, waited until all of his men went down before him, then shook hands with Col. Hobart and descended into Rat Hell himself. At the bottom of the rope ladder he waited long enough to hear Col. Hobart start replacing the bricks which closed the fireplace opening.

Rose then joined the rest of the diggers at the tunnel opening. He lined them up in the order in which they would enter the tunnel, shook hands with each man, and then went into the tunnel. Hamilton followed him.

At the end of the tunnel Rose and Hamilton came out in the shed. They brushed the dirt from their clothes, made their way to the gate, opened it, and then, when the sentry's back was turned and he was on his westward march, they strolled east on Canal Street away from Libby Prison. When they were out of sight of it they turned north. They were soon followed by the other members of the escape party, who took off in groups of two or three in all directions.

VII

In the kitchen of the prison several members of the second escape party no longer could contain their excitement and curiosity. They ran upstairs and to the east windows overlooking the vacant lot under which the tunnel had been run. They watched the tunnel-diggers emerge from the towing company building and stroll down Canal Street on their way to freedom. Other prisoners joined them at the windows and were told what was happening.

Word of the tunnel and the break now flashed through the prison. In less than a minute hundreds of men were jamming themselves against the windows, ignoring the danger, to watch the tunnel party emerge on the sidewalk and, unchallenged by sentries, disappear into the night.

A fever to escape suddenly hit the prisoners. A blind, unreasoning compulsion to break out, regardless of the consequences, possessed every man. There was a stampede to the staircases, and the men stormed down to the kitchen, jamming themselves in feverish excitement into the room where the escape passage began. They fought hysterically for the chance to squeeze into the cylindrical excavation that led through the fireplace.

Within a few minutes several hundred men were jammed into the pitch dark kitchen room, 44 feet wide by 105 feet long. Lieutenant Harry Wilcox of the 1st New York joined the rear of the pack of pushing, sweating, cursing men; he found before long, that another 200 men had jammed behind him. Once he was in the straining mob, no man could pull out, even if he wanted to. Pushed, kicked, and squeezed as he was, struggling for air, there was one mad moment when Wilcox found himself locked in a human vise, unable to move, staring through the cracks in the door on the Carey Street side at the sentry outside the prison, just 12 feet away, as he marched his beat completely oblivious to the storm that raged inside the prison.

In the front of the milling mob, the men fought bitterly for the right to jump into the opening in the fireplace. Blows were struck, noses bloodied. Men fainted from the excitement and the great pressure on their bodies from all sides—but there wasn't room enough in which to fall down. Many found it difficult to breathe and believed they were close to suffocation. Some begged to be released from the mob, but nobody listened to them. Each man was fighting his own private war.

At the fireplace opening Colonel Hobart, who had been trying to maintain some kind of order, threw up his hands and surrendered to the mob. He made one last plea to the men near him to be quiet so the sentries would not hear them, and then went into the fireplace opening himself. He was followed by Colonel T.W. West of Wisconsin. The two joined forces below in Rat Hell and entered the main escape tunnel.

As Hobart disappeared down the opening in the fireplace, a man in the rear of the mob panicked. "The guards," he screamed. "I can hear them coming!"

The prisoner was mistaken. The Confederates had no idea that an escape was in progress. But the damage already had been done. The cry of terror cut through and over all other noises in the room. For one terrible moment the mob was stilled, paralyzed, poised. Then, with an awesome rush, the dam broke. In one frenzied lunge the mob heaved and turned around—away from

63

the fireplace—toward the stairway to the sleeping rooms upstairs and what was believed to be safety, away from the dread possibility of being caught by the Confederates while attempting to escape.

In the mad rush to get out of the kitchen, men were knocked over and trampled underfoot. The staircase had no banister, and those on the outside were pushed off to fall on the struggling men below.

Outside the prison on Carey Street, one of the sentinels heard the crash of the tables and benches in the kitchen as they were knocked over. He laughed and called out good-naturedly to the next sentinel up the line: "Hey, Bill! There's somebody's coffee pot upset for sure!"

Frank E. Moran, one of the prisoners, was knocked off his feet in the first rush for the staircase. The panicked men trampled over him, their boots stamping on his head, hands, and shoulders, knocking him unconscious.

When Moran came to, he was lying in a pool of water the overflow from the kitchen sink taps. He neither heard nor saw any Confederate guards and concluded the cry of warning had been a false alarm. He crawled forward to the fireplace and dropped through the opening into Rat Hell. Landing on a swarm of squealing rats, he flailed hysterically about him in the darkness.

When he regained his feet, Moran was bewildered. He had no idea where the tunnel opening was, and it was so dark in Rat Hell he could not see his hands in front of him.

Moran stumbled around in circles until he ran into one of the walls. Putting his hands on the cold damp surface of the wall, he began to move to his right, working his way around the room as he searched for the tunnel opening. In a few minutes, he was completely lost, unaware of where he was in relation to where he had been when he entered the cellar room.

Moran had already circuited the room twice when his hands fell on a pair of boots that were disappearing into the wall. He knew then that he had found the tunnel opening. He crawled into the tunnel and started forward. After what seemed like hours of agony, he emerged in the shed, above ground, sick and faint, where he was helped to his feet by the man whose boots he had touched—Charles H. Morgan of the 21st Wisconsin. The man ahead of Morgan in the tunnel, Lieutenant William L. Watson, waited for them and together the three men walked through the towing company archway out on to Canal Street to begin the journey north.

Moran believed he had been the only one remaining behind in the pitch dark kitchen after the stampede, but he was wrong. There were other daring men on the loose that night. Lieutenant James Monroe Wells had hidden behind a kitchen stove when the mad stampede for the upstairs lofts began. Now he calmly calculated his chances. He could hear no guards coming in. "And if they do," he told himself, "they know nothing of the hole and nothing of the tunnel, and anyhow I may just as well go down and out; it can be no worse for me."

65

Wells dropped down into Rat Hell. Soon he was through the tunnel and out on Canal Street, hurrying away from the prison. On hands and knees he slipped through the fortifications and siege guns that ringed the city to the open plains beyond the city limits. Then he struck north for his goal—Chickahominy River, some six miles away.

In the kitchen that night, too, was Captain John W. Lewis of the 4th Kentucky Cavalry. A moment after the panicked stampede he found himself on the floor with four men crawling past him in single file toward the fireplace. Lewis fell in behind the last man in line and crawled forward too. In a few seconds he was going down through the fireplace opening and into Rat Hell where he and his companions searched until they found the main tunnel at the northeast end of the cellar.

The five men made it through the tunnel and left the shed as one group. They walked out on Canal Street and turned east, making their way through Richmond until they reached open country. By dawn they were hiding in a swamp on the Chickahominy, concealed from any passing Confederates by the heavy undergrowth.

That Tuesday night, February 9, 1864, the almost unbelievable total of 109 Union Army officer-prisoners found their way through the fireplace opening and escaped from Libby Prison. The last man had the presence of mind, before departing, to replace the plank that covered the tunnel exit inside the woodshed. Inside the prison itself one of the prisoners crept down to the kitchen before dawn, sealed up the fireplace opening, and camouflaged it with handfuls of soot.

By dawn of the next day the Confederates knew that one of the biggest prison breaks in all history had been made from their brick and mortar stronghold. The city of Richmond erupted in a panicked flurry of military activity. Before noon Confederate soldiers, on horse and on foot, were dispatched in all directions in pursuit of the fleeing prisoners. But only one man, Captain Gates of the 33rd Ohio, was recaptured inside the city limits of Richmond.

By noon of that day Rose and Hamilton, the first men through the tunnel, were outside the city limits and separated from each other. When they had come out of the tunnel the night before, they had walked east for a couple of blocks and then turned north. Suddenly they found themselves approaching a detail of Confederates guarding a military hospital.

Rose was a few steps in the lead. It was too late for him to turn and beat a retreat. He was already in the light of the corner gas lamps and knew the Rebel guards had seen him. He hunched his shoulders and marched forward boldly in the darkness, hoping he could bluff his way through. Behind him, Hamilton, sizing up the situation, turned and ran into a dark side street. For Hamilton there would be several days of wandering alone in the countryside once he got outside Richmond. Eventually he would stumble on a Union picket squad and be guided behind the main Federal lines.

Rose was not challenged by the hospital guards. He

walked past them, reached the Richmond city limits, and then began plodding down the tracks of the York River Railroad. By dawn he was east of the Chickahominy bridge. A half hour later he almost stumbled into a camp of Confederate calvalry.

Rose hid in the woods at the edge of the Rebel camp. He felt conspicuous in his blue Federal uniform, knowing it made travel extremely dangerous during daylight hours. As he crouched in the brush, trying to figure out what to do, his eye fell on a large hollow sycamore log. It offered a haven. Crawling inside it, he fell sound asleep.

A few hours before nightfall Rose left the log, skirted around the Confederate camp, and worked his way back to the Chickahominy River. Then he waded downstream until he found a spot where it was shallow enough to cross. In fording the river his uniform was soaked, and when he lay down in a patch of woods about an hour later, his uniform froze on his body.

All through that night Rose alternately dozed and tramped through the woods. He continued his forced march the next day, reaching New Kent Court House by late afternoon. He worked his way around several Rebel pickets, but finally was spotted by a cavalryman who spurred his horse after Rose. The Union colonel dodged into a laurel thicket. When he looked back, at least half a dozen Rebel horsemen were beating the brush for him.

Rose entered a forested area with the Rebels still after him. On the other side of the woods, at the point where he came out, he was confronted by an open field.

There was a gully through the center of this field, about a half mile long. Rose plunged into it, went down on his hands and knees, and crawled forward. He could hear the Confederates urging their horses on, calling back and forth to each other as they continued the search.

On the other side of the field Rose came out on the Williamsburg Road. He crossed into a pine forest and then fell to the ground exhausted. He slept for a while, then started on again, sticking to the woods and paralleling the Williamsburg Road. Several times he passed Confederate roadblocks without being seen, and by nightfall was at Diasen Bridge. Around midnight he could go no farther. Covering himself with pine branches and ferns, he fell into a deep sleep.

When day broke, Rose continued in the direction of Williamsburg. He believed from what he had heard in Libby before the escape that it was in the hands of Union troops. Since the territory was frequently changing hands, however, he remained cautious and kept off the roads. Whenever he came to an open field, he ran across it until he reached the next patch of woods.

Rose reached a knoll that gave him a clear view of the road to the southeast for about half a mile. In the distance he saw a body of Union troops advancing along the road in his direction. Ahead of them, were three mounted soldiers wearing Federal blue. Rose, taking them to be an advance party for the main body of Union troops, started forward to meet them. Rescue was at hand and his ordeal was finally over!

As Rose approached, the three calvarymen challenged him. He advanced slowly, suddenly unsure of himself. When he was a few yards away, the men trained their muskets on him. Rose felt he had made a terrible mistake in revealing himself.

As they moved their horses into position to hem Rose in, the three riders saw the body of Federal troops behind them. They were suddenly alarmed, and Rose realized they could very well be Confederate scouts disguised in Federal uniforms.

His worst fears suddenly became reality. The men proclaimed that they were Rebels and made Rose their prisoner. The Colonel tried to convince them he was a Confederate, too, but his captors laughed. They had no time to waste with nonsense. In a few minutes the advancing Union troops would be on them.

The Rebels split up. Two rode off while the third man started in the direction of Richmond, his musket trained on Rose, moving the Colonel along at a fast walk.

In a few minutes Rose began to limp. As soon as he and his guard were over a rise in the road and out of sight of the other two Rebels, he staggered toward his captor.

When he was close to the Rebel, Rose leaped. He got his hands on the man's musket and held on with all his strength. The horse bucked, and Rose was dragged off his feet and spun through the air. Somehow the trigger of the musket was struck, and the weapon was fired harmlessly into the air. Rose let go of the gun barrel and went sprawling. As soon as he was on his feet, he ran for the woods, reaching them before the Rebel had a chance to reload.

Rose cut back in a semicircle to the right and started running in the direction of the body of Union troops. He had gone only 20 or 30 yards when he ran head-on into a squad of Confederate troops in the woods. Leaping on him, they beat him to the ground with their musket butts.

With Rose their prisoner, the Confederates began to retreat. Taken to Richmond eventually, Rose was handed over to the authorities of Libby Prison. There he was thrown into a solitary confinement dungeon.

Rose's identity as architect of the escape and engineer of the successful tunnel was kept hidden from the Confederate authorities by his fellow prisoners. No one betrayed him.

As it turned out, the Confederates didn't know how the northern officers had escaped. From the first moment on February 10, 1864, when they learned of the breakout, the Libby Prison authorities were bewildered. All they knew was that they had lost 109 prisoners, but how or in what manner eluded them.

The prisoners who had remained behind in Libby were not helpful. They refused to talk. As for the Rebels, they rejected the mute testimony of the wooden plank that hung from a horse-blanket rope from an iron bar of the top floor southeast window.

For a number of days the mystery was complete. The Richmond newspapers carried stories about the "miraculous Yankee escape" and large crowds of people flocked to the prison and stared in open-mouthed wonder at the ominous-looking Libby building and the secret it held.

Finally, about a week after the escape, some one stumbled over the plank in the woodshed that covered the tunnel exit and the hole in the ground was exposed at last. A Negro slave was driven into the tunnel at bayonet point and told not to turn back until he came out at the other end. When he emerged in Rat Hell, the mystery of how the prisoners had gotten out was finally solved.

Of the 109 Union Army officers who fled Libby, 59 reached Union lines, 48 were recaptured, and two were drowned during the escape attempt. Those recaptured were put in the dungeons of Libby, some in chains, and kept on a diet of bread and water.

Still unsuspected of being the guiding hand behind the escape, Colonel Rose was exchanged by the Confederates on April 30, 1864, for a Rebel colonel in Union hands. On July 6, he was back with his old regiment, fighting beside his comrades. By the time the war had ended, he had been promoted to the rank of brigadier general.

Part Two
The Escape-Proof Prison

I

Wₕₑₙ Gₑₙₑᵣₐₗ Jₒₕₙ Hᵤₙₜ Mₒᵣₘₐₙ and 69 of his officers arrived at the Ohio State Penitentiary as prisoners of war on July 31 and August 1, 1863, it marked the end of a month of terror for rear area civilians in the North.

Newspaper headlines bannered daily the story of the Southern invaders who had sliced deep into Federal territory, confiscating livestock and crops, overrunning farms and small towns, even reportedly blasting open bank vaults. They had smashed resistance wherever they encountered it, threatening rear area lines of supply and communications. Many Northerners believed they would capture or raze large cities.

The terror began on the morning of July 2, 1863, when telegraph keys began to clatter across the state of Kentucky. The message was simple and blood-chilling: "Morgan the Rebel Raider is moving north. He crossed the Cumberland at dawn with 2,500 men and ten field guns."

On the march, chanting the *Song of the Raiders* and *Here's to Morgan and Duke,* the swift-moving Rebel cavalry, led by its 38-year-old general, slashed north across Kentrucky, leaving behind a trail of stunned civilians, smoking buildings, looted banks, and shattered military installations.

The raiders plundered the towns of Columbia and Lebanon in Kentucky, moved on to the Ohio at Brandenburg, where they captured two steamboats and ferried themselves across the river to enter Indiana. Then they swung northeastward through Indiana toward Cincinnati, panicking Indianapolis and the countryside as they advanced, burning mills and bridges, commandeering horses and supplies, ripping up railroad tracks that pursuing Federal troops might have used.

Ahead of the assaulting column, panic gripped Cincinnati. But the raiders, now hard-pressed by pursuing Federal troops, merely passed through that city's suburbs. As the chase grew hotter, General Morgan's plan to link up with Lee's forces invading Pennsylvania grew less capable of success with each passing day. When Lee retreated from Gettysburg, Morgan's guerillas were stranded some 300 miles from their own lines with an overwhelming Federal force prepared to close the jaws of a huge trap on them.

With their backs to the deep, turbulent waters of the Ohio, which had risen because of unseasonable rains, the Rebels were trapped at Buffington's Bar. They were ringed in on land by Federal troops and blocked off on

General John H. Morgan

the river by hastily manned Federal gunboats. What was left of Morgan's command was rapidly chopped to bits by one savage assault after another. Of the original 2,500 men with whom Morgan had started his raid into the heartland of the North, only 1,900 had reached Buffington's Bar. Of those, only two companies of the 9th Tennessee, two companies of the 2nd Kentucky, plus stragglers from all the regiments—a total of between 300 and 400 men—were able to swim their exhausted mounts across the Ohio and escape into the hill country of West Virginia. The rest were either shot, captured, or drowned in the attempt to swim the river.

Morgan's captured enlisted men were sent to regular military prisoner-of-war camps, but Northerners felt that Morgan and his officers required stronger measures. When Governor David Todd of Ohio offered to seal those "dangerous rebels" in the new "escape-proof" Ohio State Penitentiary at Columbus—a concrete, iron, and stone bastion for civilian felons—Washington accepted gratefully.

Orders for the reception of Morgan and his officers were sent out. Under the supervision of Warden Merion, a special cell block was cleared of its civilian convicts and a detail of Federal troops was assigned to the prison to join with the regular civilian prison guards in maintaining a tight security.

By July 31, 1863, Morgan and 69 of his officers began to arrive at the Ohio State Penitentiary from the Cincinnati city jail. Some came by train from the Johnson's Island prisoner-of-war camp where they had

80

MORGAN'S RAID

been held temporarily. In this latter group were the youthful General Basil Duke, Morgan's second in command, and Captain Thomas H. Hines, a slight, melancholy-appearing young man. Though he looked like a harmless youth, he had, at the age of 22, the reputation of being the "most dangerous man in the Confederacy."

The Rebel prisoners tumbled out of the cars under a savage sun and blinked grimly at their first view of the prison that awaited them. A massive stone wall, 799 feet long, 30 feet high, and 4 feet in thickness, ringed it. Along the top of the wall, guards with rifles paced between sentry boxes. The vast sweep of massive granite in view was broken only by the iron gate which now was swinging open.

Guards prodded the Rebel officers toward the yawning stone maw, through it into the prison yard, and then onto the receiving room.

If it was the purpose of the civilian prison authorities to humiliate, irritate, and anger the southern officers, they could not have mapped out a better program. The Kentucky raiders were handled like common felons in the prison receiving room. They were stripped naked, their clothes searched, their valuables, personal possessions, pocket knives, and cash confiscated by Prison Clerk Hewitt. Then they were marched naked to a washroom where two huge hogsheads of water awaited them.

Propelled by strong hands, the Confederate officers were tumbled one by one into the warm, gray water and

82

solemnly scrubbed down with large, stiff-bristled horse brushes and strong yellow soap by two Negro convicts.

The water was not changed from one bath to the next, and the twentieth man to enter it complained in a mild tone.

"Seems to me," he said, "that there water has done all it can for sanitary purposes. Ain't it got any rights?"

Next, a grinning prison barber assaulted the Confederate officers with shears and razor. Off went the pride of the men—moustaches and beards and heads of hair. Vanity and self-respect floated down with their shorn locks. In their place came a smoldering anger.

A southern colonel, D, Howard Smith, commander of the 5th Kentucky, had entered the penitentiary with a magnificent flowing beard that reached to his waist. Now, naked as a plucked chicken, he wept openly over the loss of his hair. Fellow officers tried to josh him out of his deep depression.

"It's the first time I've ever seen your face," drawled General Basil Duke. "There was no reason to hide it."
"This is no joking matter, General," the colonel replied bitterly, and turned away.

Warden Nathaniel Merion, described by contemporaries as a "rough and profane man," was on hand to enjoy the humiliation of the Rebels and make a little speech of welcome.

"You will occupy a separate cell block and separate dining tables. Any attempt to communicate with civilian inmates will bring drastic punishment." He chuckled at his own wit. "I can't let innocent convicts be contaminated by association with such hardened criminals and horse thieves as you boys, you know."

The Rebel officers were marched across the weed-studded, graveled prison yard in searing, oppressive heat. The stone prison buildings, butted together to form an inner wall enclosing the yard, seemed to cut off air as well as hope.

A guard detail crossed in front of the ragged column of prisoners. Two huge watch dogs strained at their leashes and snapped and snarled at the men. The guards laughed, and Captain Jake Bennett, 10th Kentucky Cavalry, voiced the thought of most of the Rebels: "You might as well try to escape from hell as get out of here!"

"Don't worry," Captain Hines whispered fiercely, "we'll escape. We'll pay them back for denying us exchange for Federal officers the South is holding, and for reneging on the promise of parole they gave us when we surrendered. We'll get back to the Confederacy, and General Morgan will lead us again when we get there."

But even Hines' tough determination to break out of the northern penitentiary was jarred by his first view of the granite, tomblike building in which the Rebels were to be caged. The prison authorities had cleared the southern portion of a cell block in one of the two stone-and-concrete wings of a penitentiary building to hold the Rebels. This wing was known as the East Hall. The cell block in it which had been walled off to hold the Confederate officers was little more than an oblong stone box 160 feet long, 25 feet wide, and about 40 feet high. It was roofed over with heavy sheet metal into which several skylight windows had been cut.

As the prisoners were herded through the doorway in the heavy wooden partition that had been constructed to seal them off, they were struck by the hopelessness of their situation.

Ahead of them stretched a long open hallway, about 12 feet wide, which ran the full length and height of the cell block.

On their left, on the north side of the cell block, was a windowless wall of stone cells. There were 5 floors of cells, 35 to a floor. In front of the cells on each floor was a 3-foot balcony. A short wooden ladder led from the end of each balcony to the one above it.

To the right of the prisoners was the south wall, of bleak mortar and granite blocks broken by a few barred windows close to the roof. All the prisoners could see through the windows were patches of blue sky.

Armed Federal Army guards were posted at opposite ends of the long hall, while civilian turnkeys shepherded the Rebels into their cells and locked them in. Each prisoner was isolated in his own cell.

The cells were cubelike coffins, stone-walled on three sides, with a cell door on the fourth side. They were 6 feet high, 3½ feet wide, and 6 feet deep. The doors were gratings of heavy iron bars ½ inch thick by 1¼ inch high. They were so spaced that the openings between the bars were about two inches square. Each cell contained a three-legged stool, a slop bucket, and an iron skeleton bedframe with a straw-filled tick, hinged to the wall so that it could be propped up with a stick during the day for more room. On the floor was a duckboard plank, 15 inches wide by 5 feet long.

That was the sum total of the furniture in each cell. In addition, however, most of the prisoners had carpet bags containing spare clothing. To the infinite disgust of Warden Merion, Federal General Ambrose E. Burnside had exempted the Confederates from wearing regular convict stripes or being forced to labor in the prison workshops.

Of the five tiers of cells, only the ground-floor and second-floor cells were to be occupied by the Rebel officers. As an added precaution, officers considered the most dangerous were allotted cells on the second tier. General Morgan was put in cell number 35 of the second tier, at the far or east end of the cell block, next to the wooden ladder that connected the tiers, and directly over a Federal guard post. His cell was under constant day and night surveillance. On the same tier as General Morgan and 32 other officers were Colonel Calvin Morgan, one of the General's brothers, and General Basil Duke.

On the ground floor, the inoffensive-looking youthful Captain Hines was placed in cell 20, a little more than halfway down the cell block toward the east end. In the cell immediately next to his was Colonel Dick Morgan another brother of the General's.

For the first few weeks, the prisoners were kept locked up in their individual cells except for meals and one hour of exercise in the cell block hall each day.

Hines used the long hours of confinement in his cell to try to think of ways to escape. He studied every inch of his cell for some sign of weakness, but it appeared to be impregnable. The walls were of smooth granite, the floor of concrete, without even a crack to offer hope. The door lock mechanism was set into the outer side, beyond sight or reach of the occupant.

Presently the harsh, intolerable confinement in a small cramped area was somewhat relieved. From 7 A.M. until 5 P.M. the cell doors were left open and the men permitted to visit each other and mingle in the narrow hall outside their cells, always under heavy guard. At 7:30 A.M. and again at 2 P.M., they were marched out to wash at troughs in the yard. After washing, they went into the dining hall for breakfast or dinner—the two meals of the day—which they ate separately from the regular civilian convicts. They were allowed to buy candles, and, if they wished, they could read or write letters before they turned in for the night.

Prison life fell rapidly into a pattern. To pass the dreary hours the men visited with each other, read, wrote endless letters, and played marbles in the hall. Captain Magee organized a handicraft group, and the men made trinkets from bone, lumps of coal, scraps of metal, and pieces of wood.

Hines ordered books and a chess set and made his cell the scene of a tournament that went on endlessly. As he anticipated, the guards soon grew bored at their silent concentration on the game and left the men alone to hold whispered conferences on escape plans.

"Why don't we attempt to buy our way out of here?" General Duke asked at a meeting in Hines's cell one day. "All we need is to get to one man with a bribe. God knows we can get the funds we'd need smuggled in to us by our friends in Kentucky."

General Morgan shook his head solemnly. "Too dangerous," he said. "We're being guarded by two different kinds of people—Federal soldiers and civilian turnkeys. They hate each other. Give money to one, and the other would go screaming to the authorities. They'd hang us for it."

As if to substantiate General Morgan's distrust of bribery as a means of effecting an escape, the prisoners got a harsh example a few days later in the case of Captain Foster Cheatham, who bribed a guard to buy a bottle of whiskey and smuggle it into the prison to him. A rival guard informed the authorities and Cheatham was rushed into solitary confinement. When he emerged 48 hours later, his clothes were covered with a slimey green mold and he seemed to be in a state of shock.

The solitary cell was a dark, airless iron cubicle from which even the most hardened of men emerged sick, dazed, and half-paralyzed. A day in solitary in the iron dungeon was the punishment for a wide variety of sins, including dirt on a cell floor and "jesting or boisterous talk."

The prison administration was capricious by nature, it seemed. If the authorities eased certain restrictions, allowing the Rebel officers greater physical freedom, they tightened the screws elsewhere, putting the men under severe mental torture. Always they drove the Confederates toward crossing the fine line that separates caution from desperation.

Each morning Deputy Dean inspected each cell while civilian trusties swept it out. At odd times through the day there were surprise inspections. Every two hours throughout the night a guard crept silently down the hall, holding his lamp high at each cell door, casting its light on the prisoner in the cell, frequently waking him.

Prisoners were permitted to write letters to members of their immediate families only—and no longer than one page. Both outgoing and incoming mail was censored by Warden Merion. If a letter from home displeased the warden, he confiscated it and passed the empty envelope on to the Rebel, who could then spend hours of frustrated agony examining the empty envelope and trying to figure out what news it might have contained.

Food parcels were sent to the men from their families in Kentucky. The prisoners knew about them because of what they read in the letters they got from home, but they never received the parcels. Instead, the packages piled up in Warden Merion's office and were eventually confiscated and used to supplement the warden's own meals.

"Your wife makes a delicious smoked ham," Merion once told Capt. G.C. Mullins, picking at his gums with a gold toothpick that had been confiscated at the initial shakedown of the prisoners. Mullins glared at the warden, but said nothing. Any argument would have meant 24 to 48 hours of solitary confinement in the dungeon.

The prisoners were denied visiting privileges. On one occasion General Morgan's mother, who already had lost one son in the war, came to the penitentiary to see her remaining sons. She was not permitted to talk to them. Instead, the Morgan brothers were marched out into the hall and paraded like caged animals while their mother, as a special favor granted by Warden Merion was permitted to peer through the iron bars at them.

What finally drove the men over the line and committed them to an attempt to escape—no matter how dangerous or slim its chances of success—was the dungeon they had come to fear and hate.

On a morning in October when they went in for breakfast, they found the hominy was black with filth. Major W.P. Elliott, Morgan's quartermaster, an older and kindly man whom the Rebels had come to love, complained bitterly. "Somebody must have died in the kitchen," he said. "Even the hominy has gone into mourning. It is wearing black."

A dining room guard, Isaac Hoffman, was enraged by the sarcasm and ordered Elliott into solitary confinement in the dungeon for 24 hours. The following morning, when Elliott stumbled into the dining hall after his ordeal, Hoffman came tramping over to where Elliott slumped in his place at the dining room table.

"And how do you like breakfast this morning?" Hoffman demanded.

"Fine," Elliott choked, anxious to please the guard

and avoid additional punishment in solitary confinement. "This is the best hominy I ever ate. Can I get a second helping?"

Hoffman's face darkened. "By God," he swore, "you're making fun of me!" He grabbed Major Elliott by the arms and lifted him from his seat. "For being wise, you can do another 24 hours in the pit. Then we'll see how sarcastic you are."

After the incident in the dining room, Captain Hines returned to his cell, trembling with rage. The rough and unjust treatment of Elliott was a spur in his flesh. He resolved to strike back at the prison authorities, to do something—no matter how desperate—that would even the score.

II

When Captain Hines lay down on his bunk that night he began to ponder a fantastic idea. The one possible way of breaking out of the prison had been within reach all this time, but he had not thought of it until this moment.

Their prison wing, instead of being raised on foundations, was flush to the ground, with the cell floors on a level with the prison yard. Under those conditions, the lower cells, cut off from sunlight and circulation of air, should have been damp and moldy from moisture drawn up from the earth. But such was not the case. In none of the cells on the ground level had Hines seen patches of dampness or mold.

The absence of dampness could mean only one thing. Under the cell floors there must be an air space or chamber of some kind, providing the ventilation that kept the floors dry. If that air space were deep enough to hold a man and they could get down into it, they might be able to start a tunnel unseen by the guards—and then dig through or under the building walls and thus get into the prison yard. If they could reach the yard, they would be able to scale the main prison wall. Once over that, they would be free to make their way south to the Confederate lines.

Hines was too excited with his idea to sleep that night. The first thing he did in the morning was to tap the floor of his cell with the stick normally used to prop up his bed. The cell floor sounded hollow. Hines stepped out into the hall and tapped the floor there with his stick. This time the sound was lifeless and solid. Hines was certain that his theory of an air chamber under the floors of the cells was correct.

Hurrying up to General Morgan's cell, he described his theory of an air chamber under the floor to the general.

"If I'm right," Hines said, "all we have to do is break through the floor of one cell. That would put us into the air chamber and we can start digging a tunnel from there."

Morgan nodded. "*If* you're right," he said, "we may have a chance. Pick out six men in the ground floor cells—men you can trust without question—and ask them if they want to make a try at escaping. No more than six. If we get too many involved in this, we run the risk that somebody may talk and give the whole scheme away."

Hines confided his scheme to Colonel Dick Morgan and Captains L.D. Hockersmith, J.C. Bennett, C.S. Magee, Ralph Sheldon, and Sam B. Taylor. The plan sounded good to them, too, and they were eager to start digging.

Obtaining tools for the digging proved unexpectedly easy. When two officers in the second range of cells, Lieutenant J.H. Croxton and Captain Buford A. Lacy, became ill, their meals were brought to them. Sheldon and Taylor visited the sick men in their cells. After the patients had eaten, the two would-be escapees stole the knives from their trays. Somehow Rebel luck held, and the knives never were missed.

Hockersmith, a cadaverous-looking former bricklayer, took charge of the knives. He converted them into crude hacksaws by laying them on the floor in one of the cells and hammering their cutting surfaces with the iron poker from the hallway stove. When he finished, he had a serrated edge that could bite into concrete.

Next came the problem of deciding in which cell to start the digging. If the hole were discovered by the guards, hanging might well be the reward of the cell occupant. "It was my idea," Hines said, "and I'm ready to take the risk. We'll start in my cell."

The men did not let themselves dwell too long on the almost insurmountable obstacles that must be overcome for their escape plan to succeed. Somehow the guards had to be hoodwinked and the operation kept secret. Somehow makeshift saws, serrated soft iron blades in pine block handles, had to grind through concrete of unknown depth and hardness. Each obstacle would have to be tackled in turn, with no thought to the next until it was reached.

It had been the custom for Deputy Warden Milo Scott to visit the cells each morning with a detail of civilian guards. Somehow Hines must work out a scheme to avoid the daily sweepout and inspection of his cell so that when the digging began it would not be discovered.

To begin with, Hines asked Scott for permission to buy a broom and sweep his own cell. "I'm fussy about dirt," he told the deputy warden, "and I need the exercise."

Scott gave his permission for this arrangement and Hines paid 25 cents for a broom. For a few mornings after Hines got his own broom, the deputy warden would pass Hine's cell, look into it, compliment Hines on his neatness, and then pass on to supervise the cleaning of the other cells and their inspection. Since Hines obviously was keeping his cell immaculate, Scott soon did not even make a pretense of inspecting it.

On the morning of November 2 Hines decided the pattern had been set and gave the word to begin. Hockersmith and Sam Taylor, a former carpenter and mechanic, volunteered for the arduous digging job, with the rest doing what they could to provide cover.

Hines set his stool in the doorway of his cell, ostensibly for better light, and pretended to read Gibbon's *Decline and Fall of the Roman Empire* while he kept lookout. Behind the screen of his carpet bag, Hockersmith and Taylor scratched the outline of a 14-inch square in the cement floor in the rear of the cell under Hines' cot.

To cover the rasping sound of the makeshift saws as they scraped at the cement, Magee and several other plotters hammered away with extra vigor at pieces of metal they were making into breastpins and rings. A little farther down the hallway, 200-pound Jake Bennett bellowed out his versions of songs that were popular in the regiment—"The Old Cow Crossed the Road," and "Grasshopper Sitting on a 'Tater' Vine." Whenever a guard approached, Hines coughed a warning and the diggers kicked the carpet bag over the scratches they had made on the floor, let the cot down, and sat on it.

It was a nerve-wracking day, and little progress was made. Hockersmith's report to General Morgan was not encouraging. "It doesn't look as if we've been at it all day, General," he said. "That cement is harder than rock, and our soft knives just can't do much with it. Captain Taylor didn't have much more than a vest pocketful of chips and scrapings to get rid of in the hallway stove." Still, the mere fact that they were doing something toward escape was heartening.

Succeeding days showed better results. Once past the hard surface, the crude saws hacked out chips of impressive size, and disposal of the rubble became a

problem. The diggers' pockets were bulging dangerously, and it no longer was safe to dump the waste in
the hallway stove where it might be noticed in the ash
pan.

Hines solved the problem by slitting the end of his
bed tick and stuffing the chips of cement into it. To make
room for the chips, handfuls of straw were removed,
smuggled into the hall, and burned in the stove.

The first, second, and most of the third day of digging
went by. The hole grew deeper, but there was no sign
that their task was anywhere near completion. Each
gouge, each scratch, only revealed more concrete underneath. Tapping the bottom brought no heartening
sound of a thinning shell. For all anyone knew or could
discover, the cell floor might be several feet thick. A
fear that their project was doomed to failure began to
grow in the minds of even the most optimistic of the
men.

Then, late in the afternoon of November 4, after they
had dug through 8 inches of solid concrete, the diggers
reached a subfloor made of bricks laid on end and
cemented together. For a moment, they could only
stare in dull hopelessness. Then Hockersmith leaned
down and jabbed at the mortar between the bricks with
his digging knife. The mortar flaked and crumbled
under his blows.

"Not so bad," Hockersmith whispered exultantly.
"That stuff's so soft and crumbly we could dig it out
with toothpicks! Even if we have to go through a dozen
layers of brick, if they're all like this, we'll have 'em out

97

of there in no time at all. Just chop around each brick and lift it out!"

That night Hines slept on a tick that was stuffed with bricks taken from the hole in the floor. He was too excited to mind the sharp edges that dug into his back. By noon of the next day, November 5, the diggers had removed five layers of bricks and were digging at the sixth layer when one of the bricks suddenly slipped downward and left a black opening in the bottom of the hole. They heard the brick thump somewhere below, and a current of cool, dry air blew up in their faces. By the two o'clock dinner call the rest of the bricks had been loosened and punched down, leaving a hole 14 inches square.

Hockersmith and Taylor covered the hole in the floor with Hines' carpetbag, let his bed down, and then fell out in the hall with the other Rebels for the march to the dining hall. Hines, however, stayed in his cell and called Milo Scott, the deputy warden, over. "I'm not feeling well today," he said. "I'll skip dinner and just lie here on my bunk."

"You Rebs are too delicate," Scott grumbled. "All right. But I'll lock you in until we get back."

Hines lay on his bunk and watched Scott close the cell door and lock it. He waited until the tramp of feet had died away and he was alone. Then he rolled out of his bunk, got down on his knees, and pushed the carpetbag out of the way. He held his ear to the hole. The air coming up felt musty but dry, and he could hear no sound of running water or scurry of rats. This was all to the good, but what if the hole down there was no more than a tiny niche cut out of solid rock? There was no way of knowing but what impenetrable bedrock lay just beneath the surface and that the air space it enclosed was no more than a few inches high.

Hines grabbed his bed-prop stick and probed down into the darkness of the hole with it. Incredibly, the stick reached down and down until, lying flat on the floor and stretching his arm, Hines could just reach what felt like a dirt floor.

Trembling with excitement, Hines took a stub of candle out of his carpetbag and then put his legs down into the hole. He let himself down until his feet reached a solid surface. Pulling the carpetbag over the whole form below, he crouched in the darkness and lit the candle. The yellow light flickered on a vaulted air chamber—four feet high and six feet wide immediately under his cell. It appeared to extend, in the darkness beyond the reach of his sputtering candle flame, the full length of the cell block. The floor was of soft earth, the side walls of huge granite blocks set in old mortar that looked as if it would crumble to the touch.

Hines did not dare to stay down long. Deputy Warden Scott might return to the cell block at any moment and look into his locked cell. If he did not see Hines there, knowing that he had locked him in, he would be bound to investigate.

Hines extinguished his candle and climbed back into his cell. He covered the hole in the floor with his carpetbag and lay down in his bunk. When the men

99

came back from their afternoon meal, he told them what he had seen.

General Morgan was eager to view the hole. Later that afternoon, he and Hockersmith slipped down for a more detailed examination than Hines had made. They explored the air chamber from one end to the other. It was 4 feet high directly under Hines' cell, about 1½ feet high down under the west end of the cell block, and about 12 feet from floor to ceiling at the east end. At the east end they made an interesting discovery. Hockersmith told Hines about it when they rejoined him in his cell.

"We may not even have to tunnel," Hockersmith said excitedly. "There's a wooden ventilating grating in the east end wall near the air chamber ceiling. Something's blocking the light but enough air comes in to stir a candle flame. The grating must open into a hole or well that's probably full of leaves or trash. We can pry off the grating and climb out any night."

"We'd better see what's blocking the grating first," Hines said, "before we pull it off. One mistake now could ruin everything."

Before they closed the hole with the carpetbag, the men removed the bricks from Hines' bed tick and dropped them down into the air chamber where there was plenty of room.

The next day, November 6, was one allotted to washing clothes at the troughs in the prison yard. Hines and Hockersmith finished quickly and then took a seemingly aimless stroll around the yard. They were able to get a look at the east end of their cell block wing.

Both men paled at what they saw. Piled between the east end wall and the women's wing of the prison was a mountain of coal. Prying off the grating from inside the air chamber would have made an opening through which the coal would have poured in on the men in the air chamber, betraying their secret and possibly burying them.

"That settles it," Hockersmith said glumly. "Coal on the east, the Main Hall on the west, and the whole north cell block behind us. We've got to tunnel straight south—through the stone wall of the air chamber that lies just about under your cell door—under the hallway in front of your cell—under or through the building wall—and then come up in the yard between our cell block and the prison wall. And then we'll have to figure out how to get over that!"

When they had finished washing their clothes and were marched back to the cell block, Hines and the other escapers drifted up to General Morgan's cell on the second floor. Each man had a book with him. Under cover of a supposed literary discussion, they worked out the details of the tunneling operation they were about to undertake.

It was decided that only two men would dig at a time and be relieved every hour. This would keep the guards from noticing any prolonged absence from the halls or any signs of physical exhaustion among the diggers. A signal system was worked out so that those above in the cell could keep in touch with the diggers in the air chamber below. One tap with the bed-prop stick on the floor of Hines's cell was a signal to the diggers to stop work and let another team go down in their place. Two taps was a signal that the men would have to fall out for dinner; this was to be given a half hour in advance of the dinner call. Three taps was a danger signal and meant the diggers were to stop and come up immediately.

"There is only the one hole—from your cell down to the air chamber," General Morgan told Hines. "What do we do when the tunnel to the yard outside is finished? We can only go at night—and at night the men are locked in their cells. They won't be able to reach your cell to go down into the tunnel."

Hines nodded. "I know," he said. "But there is a solution. Before we complete the tunnel, assuming that we get that far, we'll hollow out the air chamber ceiling below the cell of each man who is going out with us. We leave just a thin shell of cement in the cell floor itself. Then—on the night of the escape—each man will stamp through that half-inch shell of concrete and drop down into the air chamber."

The idea appealed to Morgan and the others. Then the General pondered the possibility of telling other men in ground floor cells about the escape plan, but finally decided against it. "Every day," he said, "increases the danger of discovery. The fewer men we have in on this will narrow the chances that somebody gives it away. If we can just get you seven men out of here, we will have struck a tremendous blow for the Confederacy."

At this point Hines interjected an issue that had been on the minds of the escape team from the first moment the plan had been conceived. "We have to figure a way," he said, "of taking General Morgan with us—or I am not going. The General is in a cell on the second floor—and locked there at night. How do we get him down on the first floor so he can go down into the air chamber with us on the night we break out?"

The escapers looked at each other uneasily. It was obvious to all that their escape would have meaning—a propaganda blow against the North—only if General Morgan escaped, too.

Colonel Dick Morgan, the General's brother, stood up and looked at the others. "Suppose you leave that to me," he said. "General Morgan is a damned sight more important to the Confederacy than I am. On the night of the escape—if we get to that point—I will exchange cells with my brother just before we're locked up for the night. He'll go into my ground floor cell, and I'll go into his upstairs. We're pretty much the same build, and I don't think the the guards will notice anything wrong."

The others agreed to this plan, and then General Morgan made one final suggestion before the meeting broke up. "From now on," he said, "everybody sleeps with his face to the wall, his hands under the blanket, and his blanket over his head. We want to get the night guards used to seeing just a faceless form in the bunks. Then—on the night we go out—we'll leave some kind of dummies behind in our places. If we're lucky we'll fool the guards and delay the discovery of our escape until morning. It'll give us that much more time."

The planning phase was over. The next morning, November 7, 1863, the actual digging of the tunnel was started in the air chamber wall immediately below Hines' cell. The men aimed their tunnel to go straight south under the door of Hines's cell, under the hallway in front of that cell, and then, when they reached it, through or under the outside wall of their cell block.

Three grueling days were spent in loosening and prying out the first big granite block, only to find more blocks behind it. It took another week to get through what turned out to be five solid feet of rock and concrete masonry.

The men broke through the other side of the air chamber wall on November 14 and started digging under the hallway in front of their cells. The first 18 inches under the hallway was fairly easy digging. It consisted of loose earth and small stones that had been used to fill in open spaces when the wall had originally been erected. But soon the earth turned into a hard tough clay which their soft iron knives could barely dent. Hockersmith managed to make connections with a civilian convict who worked in the kitchen and was able to buy a hard-steeled straight razor which he converted into a digging instrument. With this he was able to shave off the tough clay in the tunnel a stroke at a time. Still it was hard going.

Then, on the morning of November 16, the men had a fantastic stroke of luck. While washing at the trough before breakfast, Hines spied a rusty, broken-handled shovel almost hidden in the weeds of the prison yard.

He shoved his elbow into Bennett's ribs. When the captain protested, Hines nodded his head in the direction of the shovel. Bennett's eyes opened wide.

"Follow my lead," Hines said.

Hines appeared to trip and his shoulder rammed into the 200-pound Bennett's side. Bennett took a step back and then slammed into Hines. The two men started to rough-house, locking their arms about each other and wrestling. The big Bennett lifted Hines off the ground and staggered back several steps to the amusement of the guards and the other Rebel prisoners. Suddenly he seemed to trip, and fell backwards. When he landed, it was on top of the shovel. In the scramble that followed, Hines shoved the precious shovel under Bennett's coat. By the time the guards came over to break up the horseplay, the shovel was well concealed under the massive Bennett's coat. He took it to breakfast with him, and then it was smuggled down into the air chamber when the men returned to the cell block.

The tunneling through the tough, hard clay—even with the razor and shovel—was slow, agonizing work that exhausted the men. Bennett had to quit for a few days when his hands became covered with blood blisters. Even the seemingly tireless Hockersmith had to drop out for one day when he found it impossible to open his cramped fingers.

Nevertheless, inch by dogged inch the tunnel went forward, slowly and painfully, 18 inches wide by 3 feet high. The men kept it straight by sighting on a candle they burned at the tunnel mouth. One dug while another brought out the rubble in sacks made from spare shirts. Then Taylor smuggled in a small provisions box which could be pushed back and forth to handle the debris faster. For light the men donated the candles allowed them for reading in their cells and invented excuses to draw and buy more. A number went on sick call in order to steal extras from the prison hospital.

There were close calls when the tunnelers came dangerously close to being discovered. One day, when Hockersmith was digging alone, he somehow missed hearing the warning signal to come up for the afternoon meal. Either he was too far in the tunnel to hear it or the man on guard in Hines's cell forgot to give the warning.

The other prisoners were formed in line in the hallway and marched to the dining hall. At the last second, General Morgan noticed Hockersmith's absence and realized with dismay that he was still below. If the guards missed him, they would make a search and inevitably find the hole in the floor of Hines' cell and the tunnel below.

General Morgan fell out of line, muttering some excuse about not feeling particularly hungry that day. The guard shrugged. He didn't care if the General ate or not. He closed and locked the door in the partition wall at the end of the hall and hurried after the line of prisoners, leaving the General behind.

The General ran back to Hines' cell and rapped three times with the bed-prop stick as hard as he could—the danger signal to come up immediately. Then he raced back to the end of the hall, arriving there not a moment too soon.

The door opened and Milo Scott, the deputy warden, came in. He looked at General Morgan suspiciously. Hockersmith, who was coming up through the hole in the floor of Hines's cell, and out of the line of sight down the hallway, heard Scott speak.

"We just had a head count in the dining hall," Scott said suspicously. "We know you're here. But where's Hockersmith?"

"I left him on my bed a few minutes ago," Morgan said. "He wasn't feeling well. Let's go up to my cell and take a look at him. He may need the doctor."

General Morgan and Scott started up the ladder at that end of the hall to the second floor cells. As they did, Hockersmith brushed the dirt from his clothes and hurried down the hallway to his own cell on the first floor, cell number 28. He got into his bunk and pulled the blanket up over himself.

"That's strange," Scott said. "He's not in your cell, General. Come on. Lets go down and check his cell. If he's not there, I'm going to turn in an alarm."

Scott came hurrying down the ladder with General Morgan behind him. The two men marched down the hall to cell 28. Hockersmith raised his head as they walked into his cell and groaned.

"What's the trouble?" Scott asked.

"Just feeling poorly," Hockersmith said. "Didn't think I could make it into the dining hall. Is there any chance of getting something to eat in here, though?"

Scott nodded, satisfied. He left the prisoners and in a short while sent a guard with the "sick diet" of toasted bread, stewed chicken, and a cup of tea. Hockersmith stayed in his bunk until 4 P.M. when the prison doctor came in to examine him and leave some medicine. Hockersmith threw the medicine into the hallway stove when the doctor had gone, but there was no more digging that day. It had been a very close call, and the men did not want to push their luck.

As the digging of the tunnel under the hallway toward the south building wall continued, the Rebels became more and more concerned about the fact they were working blind. Although the wall of their cell block was only about two yards thick, they never had seen the prison yard on the other side. There were a few barred windows in the wall, but they were close to the roof, almost 40 feet up. Yet they had to see the prison yard. Once they had dug through the building wall, they would have to know the best place to come up inside the yard and then they would have to figure out how to get over the prison wall to freedom.

III

One day there came a chance for a look out the windows high in the south wall. A trusty brought in a ladder almost 50 feet long to work from while he brushed an accumulation of grime from the wall.

The trusty left for a few minutes and the Rebels were eyeing the ladder he had left behind when Deputy Warden Dean strolled into the cell block.

What Lay Outside the Walls?

Hines turned his back to the warden and made it appear that he did not know the warden was coming up behind him. "I have an idea," he whispered. "Play along with whatever I say." Then, in a loud voice, as Dean came up behind him: "Stop it, Sam," he said to Taylor. "I know you're strong, but not strong enough to do that."

"Do what?" Dean demanded suspiciously, glaring around him at the Rebel prisoners.

Hines pointed to the 50-foot ladder. "Sam Taylor claims he can go hand over hand on the underside of the ladder to the top, not once putting his feet on one of the rungs, and then come back down again the same way."

"You're right he can't!" the deputy warden snorted. "Even an acrobat couldn't do it!"

Taylor, an agile five-footer with abnormally long and powerfully muscled arms, caught on instantly. "I'll show you I can do it!"

Before the deputy warden could stop him, Taylor sprang at the underside of the ladder like a cat. Hand over hand, rung after rung, his body hanging straight down and away from the canted ladder, his feet never touching the rungs, he scurried up. At the top, he paused to rest for a few moments before making the descent. Almost by coincidence, it seemed, he rested at one of the windows high in the south wall. He had a clear and unobstructed view of the prison yard, and he made a careful study of it with the trained, professional eye of a soldier.

After a couple of minutes the deputy warden became

uneasy and called Taylor down. Taylor descended swiftly. The moment the Rebels were alone, Taylor reported on what he had seen. "On your left as you look out," he said, "there is a double wooden gate. The inside one is made of wooden pickets, and it's about 20 feet high. The gate is hinged on the women's cell block on our east—and it runs from there to the outside wall. If we had a rope and a grappling hook, we could haul ourselves up on top of that picket gate, and then go from that to the top of the outer wall."

Captain C.C. Morgan volunteered to make a 35-foot climbing rope, using old towels and strips of mattress covers. He would make it in links so they could climb it easily. When they were ready to go out, Sam Taylor would bend the stove poker into a grappling hook which they would tie to the end of the rope.

Meanwhile, the men figured they would have to get cash for railroad tickets and other supplies they would need if they managed to escape. General Morgan had a few dollars tucked in a boot, but it was not nearly enough. Hines wrote a letter to his sister in Kentucky, asking her to send him a box of books with Federal currency pasted inside the covers. For ten dollars an old trusty mailed the letter outside the prison. In time the money arrived safely.

On November 21 the tunnel reached the 6-foot thick outer building wall. Beyond lay soft earth and freedom—if nothing went wrong. So far, despite emergencies and one or two near-disasters, their luck had been remarkably good.

111

In four days of digging the men went through the outer building foundation wall and burrowed into the earth of the prison yard outside their cell block. On November 25 they angled up and then stopped digging when they came within 2 feet of the surface. Those last 2 feet were left for the night they would attempt their breakout.

As the tunnel approached completion, the diggers turned to the task of undercutting the cell floors so that the escapers would be able to stamp through them and get down into the air chamber. This posed a serious problem in measurement. The floor of each escaper's cell had to be located exactly in the air chamber ceiling from underneath.

Again Hines tricked the deputy warden into unwittingly aiding them. By starting a noisy argument over the exact length of their hallway, he got Dean to bring in a measuring line to prove to Hines just how wrong he was. When the deputy warden had made his point, Hines reeled in the measuring tape for him while General Morgan kept him occupied. Hines used the line to get the exact distance between the centers of adjoining cells and to mark off his bed-prop stick in feet and inches. With Hines' cell as a base, measuring with the stick, it was an easy matter to locate the other cells in the air chamber ceiling and start cutting up into the floors.

On November 26 Hines bribed a trusty, an older man named Heavy who was permitted to run errands outside of the prison for the authorities, to bring him a pint of French brandy and a newspaper. The train schedules, which were listed in the papers, were essential to their plans.

They had intended to try to reach Canada, but the railroad timetable ended that hope. No trains were scheduled to reach the border until mid-morning. Long before then the escape would have been discovered and border guards alerted to stop them. The only alternative was a train leaving the local station at 1:15 A.M. and going South. If it were on time, it would enable the escapers to reach Cincinnati before the cells were opened in the morning—at which time they expected their absence to be discovered. The Rebels figured that this schedule, although tight, would enable them to cross over into Kentucky before daylight and take refuge with Confederate sympathizers. Since the night guard usually made his rounds at midnight, they figured they would go down into the airchamber shortly after that, which would allow them enough time to make the 1:15 A.M. train.

All they were waiting for now was a night of foul weather when the guards would be holed up in one of the buildings and the dogs, which ordinarily roamed the yard at night, would be penned in their kennels.

November 27 dawned bright and clear and the escapers voted against a breakout attempt that night as too dangerous. Then, later in the day, they heard news that made them change their minds. A new general was on his way to replace General Mason, the military commander at Columbus. Morgan knew what that would

mean. "His first move will be to inspect his new command, and that will include us and our quarters.
They're sure to discover the hole in the floor of Hines'
cell."

"That doesn't leave us much choice, does it?" Hines
said.

"None at all," Morgan snapped. "No matter what the
weather is like, we go out tonight!"

About 5 P.M. the sky began to cloud. It seemed that
Rebel luck was still holding; and the weather might yet
be foul enough to aid the escape attempt.

Just before lock-up time Hines went the length of the
hallway, sprinkling fine coal dust on the floor in front of
the cells. It made a fine crackling noise underfoot and
was intended for the night guard who made his rounds
at ten, midnight, and three in the morning. He had a
habit of sneaking quietly from cell to cell, flashing his
lamp on the inmates, hoping to catch them in some kind
of mischief. On this of all nights the Rebels did not want
to be taken by surprise.

Lock-up time finally came. Milo Scott, the deputy
warden, rapped on the hallway stove to signal the men
to go to their cells for the night. In the confusion made
by the milling about of the men as they went to their
cells, two events went unnoticed by the guards. First,
Sam Taylor picked up the stove poker and slipped it
under his jacket before going into his cell. As soon as it
was dark enough he would bend it into a grappling
hook and tie it to the climbing rope Captain C.C.
Morgan had made. Second, General Morgan stepped

114

into his brother's cell, number 21 on the first floor, and Colonel Dick Morgan went up to the second range of cells and entered number 35, the general's cell. Both kept their backs to the cell doors while they were being locked in, and the guards did not notice what had happened.

Then before the Rebels could congratulate themselves on successfully accomplishing the first steps of their plan, something went wrong. A guard came down the hall toward cell 21 looking for Dick Morgan and stopped at the cell door. The General kept his back to him and waited tensely—afraid that at any moment he would be challenged and dragged out of the cell.

"Your saw wasn't turned in," the guard said. The men had been issued a number of small handsaws that day for their handicrafts and jewelry-making. It seemed that the one Dick Morgan had drawn now was missing. General Morgan silently cursed his bad luck—and his brother's slip.

In each cell the Rebels waited tensely for the guard to discover he was talking to General Morgan and not Dick Morgan—and thus blow the whole escape scheme. Then, down the hall, the prisoner in Cell 4, Captain Thomas Bullitt, cleared his throat and called out: "Major Higby borrowed that saw. He's up on the second tier—in number 6."

The guard walked down to the end of the hall, climbed the ladder, walked past the cell where Dick Morgan was hiding in the general's cell, and then down to number 6 where he confiscated the missing saw.

After that the cell block appeared to settle down for the night. The sounds of heavy, even breathing and muted snoring filled the block. One man prayed without a break, his voice a low monotone that beat like waves against the walls. At ten o'clock the night guard came crunching over the coal dust, swearing at the noise and flashing his lamp into each cell. A little before eleven, a heavy storm broke and rain lashed against the cell block walls and drummed on the metal roof.

At midnight the guard made his rounds again, the coal dust crackling under his boots. As soon as he had completed his turn and disappeared behind the partition wall at the end of the hallway, the seven escapees were set for action.

Each rose from his bunk and set about creating a dummy to take his place. Stool, bucket, extra clothing, even loaves of bread that had been donated by other Rebel prisoners from their precious hoards, were dumped in an elongated mound on each cot and then covered with a blanket to simulate a sleeping prisoner. Each man dressed, then pulled on a second pair of trousers and his gray uniform jacket. These would be discarded after the crawl through the muddy tunnel, leaving the clothes beneath clean and nondescript enough to arouse no suspicion outside.

Sam Taylor, the powerful little captain who had climbed the ladder using only his hands, was the first to start by prior agreement. As soon as he was convinced that all was normal in the cell block and the guard was gone, he stamped through the thin shell in his cell floor.

Picking up his bag, he let himself down through the hole into the air chamber. Without wasting a moment, he walked the length of the air chamber, stopping only long enough to tap on the cell floor of each of the escapers to signal them that all was clear and to come down.

Each man broke through the undercut shell in the floor of his cell and descended, making his way across the air chamber to the tunnel entrance by the gloomy, flickering light of Taylor's candle stub. Hockersmith went into the tunnel first, taking the shovel with him, and the others crawled after him.

At the head of the tunnel, Hockersmith went to work, carefully chopping away at the last two feet of earth that separated him from the surface. He had to stop frequently so that the man behind him could clear away the dirt that piled up around his feet. The dirt was pushed back from man to man and distributed the length of the tunnel.

About 20 minutes after he had started carving at the end of the tunnel, Hockersmith saw a small opening and felt a draft of cool air. He had broken through to the surface. He put his hand up through the hole and rain beat against his hand.

"We're through," Hockersmith whispered exultantly to the man behind him, and the word was passed down the tunnel.

In a few minutes Hockersmith opened the hole wide enough so that he could crawl through. He crouched in the rain and looked around the prison yard. All was quiet. There were no guards to be seen, the dogs were in their kennels. Satisfied that the coast was clear, he put his head to the opening and called to the other men to come up out of the tunnel.

They had surfaced near the cell block wall. Now, at a half-crouch, they ran along the wall until they reached the wooden gate that was hinged to the women's cell block wing. Taylor climbed the gate, using its cross-braces as footholds, and fixed the climbing rope to one of the pickets on top. The others swarmed to the top, using the loops in the rope as footholds, and the last man pulled the rope up after him.

At the end of the gate, the men boosted themselves onto a wing wall, ran along it, and scrambled the last few feet to the top of the main wall of the prison, 30 feet above the ground.

In an empty sentry box on top of the wall the men pulled off their muddy outer clothing. During the day this sentry box was occupied by a guard, but at night the guards were inside the prison and at the main gate.

General Morgan spotted a rope running along the outer edge of the top of the wall and cut it. The rope was a primitive alarm device which was connected to a bell in the warden's office.

Fixing the grappling hook to an iron rod embedded in the top of the wall, they dropped the climbing rope to the ground outside of the prison. One after another they went down it, using the loops as steps. They alighted about 60 yards from a bend in the prison wall, just out of sight of prison guards squatting around a fire.

The escapers were about to pair off and split up when General Morgan missed his carpet bag. He realized he had left it behind in the prison yard when he climbed the gate. Hockersmith and Taylor climbed the rope once more, went back over the prison wall and into the yard to get it. When they rejoined the others they tried to disengage the climbing rope, but the grappling hook was fixed solid and would not come free. So they left it hanging against the prison wall.

IV

The tracks of the Little Miami Railroad ran parallel to the prison wall. General Morgan and Captain Hines decided to walk down these tracks to the railroad depot in Columbus. Hockersmith and Bennett would follow them after an interval of a few minutes, and Taylor and Sheldon after them. Magee, who was going to try to reach his home in West Virginia, would go in a different direction. He wished the others luck, waved good-by, and disappeared in the darkness.

After a short walk, Hines and Morgan reached the depot. There was a train on the tracks getting up steam. While Hines went to buy two tickets to Cincinnati, Morgan approached the conductor who was standing on the platform. The time was slightly after 1 A.M.

"Is this the train for Cincinnati?"

The conductor nodded.

"Will it be leaving soon?"

"It's scheduled to leave in another fifteen minutes,"

the conductor said. "There are some more cars that are supposed to join us, but they haven't come in yet."

Morgan was apprehensive. He wanted to get away from Columbus and the penitentiary as quickly as possible. There was no way of knowing when their escape would be discovered, and the first place the prison authorities were bound to look was the railroad depot.

"Are you going to wait for the other cars?"

"No. As soon as my train is ready, we're pulling out."

Morgan felt a surge of relief. He joined Hines, and the two stood in shadows in the depot and waited as the minutes slowly passed. Finally the train started to move. They sprinted for it and jumped aboard.

Standing on the rear platform of a coach, they checked the car before they entered it. Hockersmith and Bennett sat together, pretending to be asleep. In front of them was a major in the uniform of the Federal Army.

"There may be a train check," General Morgan said, "and we have no passes or permits to travel. I'll sit with the major. Maybe they'll pass us by if they see me talking to him. You sit right behind us and act as if you're a part of our party. Better let me have the pint of French brandy you paid Heavy to bring in to the prison with the newspaper. It'll help get the conversation going with the Major."

Hines went to his seat first. The General followed and sat next to the Federal officer. Morgan started talking to the Major and then broke out his bottle of brandy. Each man took a healthy swallow.

The train was rolling at a steady speed now and passing the penitentiary. Hines peered out the window and could have sworn he saw their escape rope hanging down the outer prison wall, swaying in the breeze.

The Major gestured towards the penitentiary. "That is where the Rebel General Morgan is being kept," he said.

Morgan looked past the Federal officer at the dim outlines of the penitentiary. "Yes," he said, "and I hope they keep him as safe as they've got him now."

As the train rolled through the night, General Morgan and the Federal major alternately dozed and talked. At Dayton the train was stalled for over an hour by an obstruction on the track. This meant trouble for the escapers. The plan had originally called for them to be on another train out of the Cincinnati station before the 7 A.M. morning fallout for breakfast and roll call at the penitentiary when they were certain their escape would be discovered. Because of the delay at Dayton telegrams might already be out and the railroad station in Cincinnati swarming with Federal troops looking for them.

It was well past the 7 A.M. deadline—and the escape had already been discovered back at the penitentiary and a huge dragnet thrown out, although the fleeing Rebels had no way of knowing this—when the train began to pull into the outskirts of Cincinnati. Morgan,

Hines, Hockersmith, and Bennett met on the car platform. Sheldon and Taylor were nowhere to be seen.

"We can't make it into Cincinnati in time to catch the
train we wanted," Hines said. "If we stick with this train
and go into the depot we may be trapped."

"We're not going into the station," Morgan said.
"We're getting off right here. I know some Confederate
sympathizers in this area who will give us shelter and
then pass us on." He turned to Hockersmith and Bennett. "You men had better come with us."

Hockersmith looked at Bennett and then shook his
head negatively. "We've already talked this over," he
told Morgan. "We're going to take our chances with the
train all the way. We have through tickets to Coving-
ton, and we'll cross the Ohio River that way—if our
luck holds."

Near Ludlow Ferry on the Ohio, Morgan and Hines
yanked the train's energency cord. The train ground to
a shuddering halt. The two jumped clear of the train
and landed on the road bed incline, just a few yards
from a Federal Army supply dump. Behind them the
train started moving again.

Two Federal Army soldiers, taking a break on a pile
of lumber, watched the two men land. They tossed their
cigarettes away, got to their feet, and raised their rifles.

"Why jump off the train here?" they demanded.

Morgan and Hines stopped dead, and then Morgan
decided to try to bluff it out. "What's the sense of riding
all the way into town," he growled, "when we live out

here? And for that matter, what business is it of yours where we get off the train?"

Under the lash of his commanding voice, the soldiers mumbled sheepishly and lowered their guns. The two walked past the soldiers down to the Ludlow Ferry landing where they found a boy with a skiff. For a two-dollar fee the boy rowed them across the Ohio and left them in front of the home of Mrs. Ludlow, known to General Morgan as a reliable Confederate sympathizer. When they knocked, and a servant came to the door, General Morgan took out a blank card and dashed off a note, short and to the point. "General Morgan and Captain Hines, Escaped," he wrote, and then sent the card in. A few minutes later the two Rebel officers were sitting down with the Ludlow family to a breakfast of steaming coffee and hot rolls.

The two escapees were supplied with fresh horses and a pair of pistols each, then were guided southward through Kentucky from the home of one Confederate sympathizer to the next. They had to be very careful. Federal scouts under Jerry Boyle were scouring the countryside for the escapees and had already captured two. Captains Taylor and Sheldon had been picked up six miles outside of Louisville and started on the road back to solitary confinement in the penitentiary in Columbus.

At 2 A.M. on December 1 a guide took Morgan and Hines across the Kentucky River at the ferry on the road to New Castle in Henry County. Beyond this point he

123

did not know the roads or who were Confederate sympathizers. Turning around, he left Morgan and Hines to make their own way.

In the early hours of the morning the two approached a house on the main highway leading from the ferry. Hines pounded on the door until they heard a stirring inside and a man came sleepily to the door.

"We'd like to spend the rest of the night in your house, if we may," Morgan said. "We've been on the road since early this morning."

The man nodded and stepped aside to let them enter. Then he closed the door behind them and led the way into the living room where a kerosene lamp burned on a center table. Hines spotted a copy of the *Cincinnati Enquirer*, a Democratic paper, lying on the far side of the table. On the basis of what he knew of the newspaper, Hines believed it indicated that the man might be a Confederate sympathizer.

Hines picked up the paper. Black headlines told the story of the escape from the Ohio State Penitentiary. "I see," Hines said, "that General Morgan, Hines and other Rebel prisoners have escaped from the Yankees."

The man smiled. "Yes, and you are Captain Hines, aren't you?"

"Yes. And what is your name?"

"Pollard."

"Then, Mr. Pollard," Hines said, half-turning and nodding his head in the direction of the general, "allow me to introduce General Morgan."

124

Hines had made no mistake. Pollard was a Confederate friend. They could take their fingers off the triggers of the pistols concealed in their pockets. They were made welcome, given beds in which to rest for a few hours, and then given a hearty breakfast.

At Pollard's suggestion, the two agreed to pose as cattle buyers. He furnished them with cattle whips and they went on south to the home of Judge W. S. Pryor, outside New Castle, and from there on to Shelbyville. Always they moved south toward the Confederate lines. They crossed the Cumberland, Obey's River, and finally reached the Tennessee River on December 13 about 15 miles below Kingston at Bridge's Ferry. There they gathered 40 men of Morgan's command who had been wandering about and living off the country since the defeat at Buffington's Bar.

That December morning Morgan and Hines squatted on the banks of the Tennessee and gauged their chances of crossing the river and working their way farther south. They had no boat with which to make the crossing. The river was high, its water flowing swiftly, and was about 150 yards wide at that point.

The two swung onto their horses to survey the neighboring countryside. When they stopped at a house, a man and woman came to the door and stared at them suspiciously.

"We have a shipment of beef cattle," Hines said, "for some Federal troops in this area. Can you tell us where they are?"

Some of the suspicion left the man's face. "That must be the Federal cavalry camp you want," he said. "They're just two miles down river of here."

Hines shuddered inwardly. He had visions of the General and himself blundering into the middle of a Federal Army camp and being captured within a few miles of Confederate lines.

Hines off-saddled and picked up a gleaming, long-handled axe in the yard. "Pay you ten Federal dollars for this," he said, "for just a few hours, and then leave it for you down at the river."

The man nodded. Hines left the greenbacks on the stack of firewood and swung up on his horse with the axe in hand. He and the General turned their mounts and rode back to the river.

As soon as they reached the river Hines gave the axe to their men and put them to work. He had them fell trees, peel them into logs, then split the logs and bind them together to make a raft on which they could cross the river, swimming their horses behind.

A crude yet workable raft was ready in less then an hour, and the river crossing began. Three hours later, when Morgan, Hines, five horses, and 25 men had crossed over on the raft, fifteen men still were waiting to cross when Federal troops appeared, captured them, and opened fire on Morgan's party across the river. Under fire the Rebels scattered into the hills on foot. Morgan, Hines, and three who had mounts whipped their horses over a spur of the mountain ahead of them and descended by a bridle-path to a ravine on the other side.

The country was unfamiliar to them, and they needed a guide. Hines spotted a log cabin about a hundred yards up the ravine. "I'll take a look," he told Morgan, "and see if I can get somebody to lead us over the mountains. I'd better go alone. No telling where the Federals are in this area."

He rode to the cabin where he found a woman and several children. She could not go herself, but was willing to let her 10-year-old son accompany Hines and show him the way.

As Hines swung the youngster up behind him in the saddle, he heard the clatter of hoofs in the ravine. Then a group of about 75 Federal cavalrymen came into view, heading in the direction of the spot where Morgan and his men sat their mounts in thick underbrush.

Hines knew the cavalrymen had seen him and there was no chance of escaping. What he feared now was that they might spot Morgan and capture him too.

Hines lifted the boy to the ground. Then he dug his spurs into the flanks of his horse and galloped for the advance point of the column of Federal cavalry. The column's commanding officer came riding to meet him.

"Hurry, Major!" Hines cried as he rode up. "There's a party of Rebels rode by this way just a few seconds ago."

"The Federal officer reined his mount in and looked at Hines suspiciously. "Who are you?" he demanded.

"I'm a member of the Home Guard Company in this area," Hines said. He pulled his rearing horse around and sank his spurs into its flanks. The horse bolted and clattered down the ravine at full gallop—away from the spot where Morgan and his men were concealed. "Hurry," Hines shouted, "or they'll escape!"

The Union Army officer whipped his horse in hot pursuit after Hines. His column of troops took off after him and was soon strung out along the ravine thundering at full gallop.

After about a half mile of wild riding that seemed to be bringing them no closer to any fleeing Rebels, the Union officer was certain that something was wrong. He hailed Hines and ordered him to come to a halt.

Just ahead of the two horsemen, as they reined in, was a mud slide across the ravine, brought down from the hills by the morning's rain. The hot sun had dried it into a flat mud cake, barren of any hoof marks. It was obvious, both to Hines and the Major, that no riders had passed this way since morning.

The Union major was aware he had been tricked. Unbuttoning his holster, he took his pistol out and rested its barrel on the top of his saddle pommel.

"Just *who* are you?" he demanded.

"A member of General Morgan's command." Hines grinned. "No point in concealing it any longer." He decided to hide his identity. If the Yankees did not realize he had escaped from the Ohio prison, they might be careless with him. His underwear belonged to a Rebel prisoner at the penitentiary named Bullitt, and Bullitt's name was stitched on it. "I'm Captain Thomas Bullit," Hines said.

"And what you did," the Federal officer said bitterly, "was trick me from General Morgan. I probably had

128

him trapped there back at the head of the ravine. I know it was Morgan because he was recognized at the house where you borrowed an axe."

The major's fury mounted at realization of the magnitude of the prize that had slipped through his fingers. "If I'd taken Morgan," he said, "they'd have given me a brigadier's commission and a $5,000 reward. This way I get nothing. And it was your doing. For that, my friend, you're going to pay."

The major turned to a sergeant. "Put a rope around his neck," he said, "and string him up from a tree."

The noose was knotted quickly and dropped around Hines' neck. His horse was jockeyed into position under a tree and the free end of the rope thrown over a thick overhanging branch. The sergeant pulled the rope tight, lifting Captain Hines upright in the saddle.

"Just a moment," Hines choked. "I want to say something."

The sergeant looked over at the Yankee major. The latter nodded his head. "Let him speak," he said, "and then be damned quick about it."

"Let's say that was General Morgan back there, as you say it was," Hines said. "And that I led you astray so that he could escape."

"That is exactly as I see it," the Union major said.

"Then," Hines said, "if that is the way things are, and I am a member of General Morgan's command, would I not deserve to hang if I had not done what you charge me with?"

The Union officer stared thoughtfully at Hines for a

moment. The expression on his face finally changed to one of wry amusement. He knew that the Rebel had tricked him, and that hanging him for doing his duty would gain nothing.

The major turned to his men. "By God, boys," he said, "he's right. Let him alone. Take the rope off his neck."

Hines was placed under guard while the Union major and most of his men scoured the countryside for Morgan. But the General had used the time gained by Hines' ruse to good purpose. He already was making his way over the mountains, and a few nights later was in Franklin, North Carolina, safely inside Confederate lines.

While Morgan was being feted with joyous celebrations by the Confederates, Hines was a prisoner again. He was locked in a log cabin barracks in an encampment of the 3rd Kentucky Federal Infantry just outside of Lowdon. In the cabin with him were three of the men who had been captured on the North side of the Tennessee River on December 13.

There were also three Yankee guards in the cabin. From them Hines learned they were supposed to be taken to General Burnside's headquarters in Knoxville, Tennessee, the next morning. Hines was sure he would be recognized there and placed under such strict guard that he never would have a chance to escape again.

Taking his fellow prisoners aside, he persuaded them to attempt a break with him that night. A few hours before dawn their chance came. When clouds darkened the moon, Hines and the three Rebels left their bunks, gathered around the stove, and started swapping stories with the Yankees about their combat experiences. As they talked, Hines drifted slowly to the door.

"We were cut off at Buffington's Bar," one of the Rebels was saying. "And it looked as if your cavalry was going to chop us up and drive what was left of us into the river when—"

At that moment Hines lifted the latch, threw open the door, and dashed into the darkness. His fellow Rebels tried to follow, but the guards quickly barred their way and backed them against the wall at bayonet point.

Hines crouched and sprinted through the startled guards near the hut. They opened fire on him, but missed, and he had reached the edge of the camp clearing when he ran head-on into a sentinel. As he dodged away, the startled guard brought up his rifle and fired. Hines was so close he felt the heat of the muzzle blast, but the lead ball whistled past his ear.

Hines ran as fast as he could along a road. Behind him, on the dead run, came the sentinel who had fired and missed.

Sprinting around a bend in the road, Hines flung himself into underbrush and watched the sentinel run past. Then he scrambled up a mountainside, reaching its crest by dawn, and hid in a pastureland of dead grass.

As the day passed, he heard searching parties of Federal soldiers pass within a few steps of where he lay concealed and listened as they talked about where they might find him.

When night fell, Hines came out of hiding and began walking south. For eight days he traveled by night, taking his course by the stars, holing up in the mountains and sleeping during the day, scavenging for food as he went. On December 27, 1863, he reached the Confederate lines near Dalton, Georgia, his long journey to freedom finally at an end.

Of the seven Rebels who had broken out of the Ohio State Penitentiary, only two men, Taylor and Sheldon, were caught and returned to solitary confinement. General Morgan, Captains Magee, Hockersmith, Bennett, and Hines all made it safely back to the Confederacy.

Part Three
"There Goes Sergeant Benson!"

I

JOHN W. JONES WAS A free man and a highly respected Negro citizen of Elmira, New York. His job was burying people. Or, as he preferred to put it, his profession was that of undertaker. He performed his tasks efficiently, properly, inexpensively.

But Sexton Jones, as he was called, never would have accumulated the fortune that made him one of the wealthiest Negroes in New York State if there had not been a Civil War and if the Federal Government had not decided to open a Confederate prisoner of war camp for enlisted men in Elmira. The Federal Government contracted to pay Sexton Jones $2.50 to bury each Rebel prisoner who happened to die in the camp.

As it happened, a great many prisoners died there. No one knows for sure how many. The official death toll was 2,963. But most prisoners believed it actually was much higher. For the Elmira prison camp was a blot on the Union, a corner of Hell on earth.

At Elmira about 10,000 prisoners were jammed at a time into an area of less than 29 acres. The sewage system broke down, if it ever existed, and a pond in the center of the camp became a liquid cesspool, a dump for garbage, a breeding ground for disease.

The rations scarcely kept a man alive. Fruit and vegetables were almost nonexistent. A meal might consist of a bit of beef from which a prisoner must pick the maggots. Scurvy was prevalent, causing men's teeth to fall out and pus sores to form on their bodies. It was no wonder the men took to killing rats for food and haunting the garbage piles for a scrap of sun-baked bone.

No cruelty is as extreme as that meted out by men with absolute power in their hands. Prison guards at Elmira were no exception to that rule. Prisoners were struck for little reason or thrown into solitary confinement on a diet of bread and water. Worst of all was the "sweat box," a wooden contrivance seven feet tall, 20 inchs wide and 12 inches deep, in which a prisoner could scarcely breathe as he cooked under a blazing sun. Every once in a while prisoners were shot down like mad dogs.

Yet the worst place in the camp was the Dead-House where Sexton Jones carried out his duties—as various prison authorities attested—in a "faithful," "proper," "busy," and *"reverent"* manner. The Dead-House seemed hotter than the tents and barracks in summer and colder in winter, its flies more numerous, its stench more powerful, its inhabitants more transient.

Sergeant Berry Benson

In one three-month period in the camp, 775 of 8,347 Rebel prisoners—or 9 percent—died of disease or malnutrition. In another month 495 bodies passed through the Dead-House, and on one day of that month there were 48 burials in a newly created cemetery on the outskirts of Elmira where Sexton Jones kept count of the graves.

Confederate burial details, stripped to the waist and their bodies slimed with sweat, placed the dead in pine coffins and nailed down the lids. Then civilians hired by the Government under Sexton Jones' direction drove the dead (no more than six to one wagon) out of the camp on their last ride. Occasionally the Union Army surgeon in charge of the pest-hole performed an autopsy under a tent in view of the living.

One afternoon a Rebel coffin-maker hunched over in a corner of the Dead-House so that no one could observe what he was doing. Nervously he counted a wad of Federal greenbacks and then stuffed them into a pants pocket. Turning, he stared thoughtfully at the body in the next coffin he had to work on—that of a big, powerful man, 6 feet tall and still heavily fleshed in spite of the meager camp diet. He nodded to himself and then carefully selected a lid with a slight warp to it. Whn he laid it on top of the coffin containing the big man, the closure was not perfect. Then he took a hammer and nails and worked his way around the lid, driving the nails in, but making sure that none went home all the way. There was play between the lid and the coffin, and it was possible for fresh air to get inside to the body in the pine box.

Another Rebel undertaker poked his head inside the Dead-House and asked, "Got many more?"

"No," the carpenter said. "Just this last one. Give me a hand and we'll load him up."

The two men raised the pine coffin to their shoulders straining under their burden, and carried it out to the dead wagon. When the first man stumbled and slipped, the coffin-carpenter yelled anguishedly, "Be careful! What do you want to do—dump a dead man on the ground?"

"What difference does it make?" the other growled. "If it opens up, we can always nail the lid back down. Or if it breaks open, we can put him in another one. It doesn't make any difference to him anymore."

"Have respect," the carpenter said. "It may be you quick enough."

They steadied the load on their shoulders and carried it the rest of the way to the dead wagon. They slid the box carefully into place on top of the other coffins, then stepped back. The wagon driver looked at them questioningly. The Confederate carpenter raised his hand, signaling the driver to move out—and the driver nodded and clucked to his horse.

There were one or two false starts as the horse put its weight against the traces. The dead wagon rocked in the ruts, and for a moment there was danger the topmost coffin might slide off and burst open on the ground. The Dead-House carpenter stared in horror, unable to turn his eyes away from impending disaster. Then, finally, the wheels rode up over the ends of the ruts and the wagon started to move.

The dead wagon creaked its way north along the short spur that tracked between the pond and the stockade fence. Then it made a right turn and soon passed the three wooden buildings where the camp's 16 Federal police sergeants slept. These men were entrusted with maintaining order and ferreting out tunnels and other escape attempts. On the main road that led to the camp gates the driver reined in his horse and took a long look at the camp.

Beyond the fetid pond was the smallpox hospital, and beyond that the stockade fence. On the farther side the Chemung River flowed parallel to it. Forty yards to the east of the smallpox ward were the makeshift hospital tents which had been thrown up when scurvy hit the Rebels. Near the pond were deep pits into which the cooks threw garbage; there the ever hungry Rebels foraged for bones which might still have a bit of meat, no matter how ripe. Near the pits were a few fires over which several prisoners broiled the rats they had killed and skinned. The camp abounded with rats; they swarmed under the cookhouses and in burrows along the banks of the pond. They were considered a "Chinese delicacy" by the prisoners, and a heavy trade was done in them for coffee, crackers, tobacco, and greenbacks.

The driver flicked his whip over his horse and the cart creaked on—past the prison commandant's office, and finally, after being checked by the guards, through the camp gates and onto West Water Street.

About half an hour later, as the wagon moved slowly through the open countryside, the driver heard a strange squeaking noise. Then there came a sound like that of wood splintering. The horse seemed to stop of its own accord as the driver looked around, eyes wide in terror.

The lid of the topmost coffin was wrenched up and a big man wearing a Confederate uniform sat up slowly, drawing a splinter of wood from the palm of one hand.

The man mopped at his sweating face with a huge handkerchief, then climbed out of the coffin. Ignoring the driver, he put the lid back on the coffin, realigning the splintered pieces, and then hammered the nails back in as far as he could with the heel of his hand. He drove the nails the rest of the way in by stamping them down with the heel of a boot. At last he sprang to the road and walked to the front of the wagon. He looked up at the driver, who stared back, open-mouthed.

"Now listen to me carefully," the big man said. "Don't ever dare tell anybody what you seen out here today. You just put it out of your mind. Don't breathe a whisper of it back at the prison camp. Because if you do"—he leaned forward, locked both hands on the shirt-neck of the driver, and drew his face close—"if you do, why then I'm going to come back here and kill you. You just take that empty coffin out to the cemetery and bury it there just like there was a body in it. Bury it with the rest of them coffins you got on your wagon."

The driver nodded numbly, and the big man let him fall back in his seat. Then he stepped back several paces, spun around, and loped off into the woods that bordered the country road.

The Confederate prisoner-of-war who had escaped

141

the Elmira prison camp by riding out inside a coffin was a Georgian known to his fellow inmates only as "Buttons" because of his curious gray coat. On it he had sewed brass buttons which he had taken in the field from the uniforms of dead Union soldiers. Somehow he had managed to have a supply of Federal greenbacks smuggled to him in Elmira. With this money he had bribed a Dead-House carpenter, a soldier from Mississippi, to enclose him in a coffin.

No one knows today whether the prisoner called "Buttons" ever made his way back safely to the Confederacy. But the story of his escape became common knowledge in the stockade and the Union guards took added precautions. No matter how easy it looked, Elmira was a most difficult prison from which to escape.

But a smart, tenacious Rebel prisoner named Sergeant Berry Benson was one of those who did not believe it.

II

On July 25, 1864, when Sergeant Berry Benson of the 1st South Carolina Volunteers was marched in with other prisoners, the Elmira P.O.W. Camp was a far cleaner, healthier spot than it was to become. There were only 5,000 prisoners in the stockade then—a number that was soon to double and more.

Benson was barely 20 years old when he arrived at Elmira. He had enlisted at the age of 17 at Charleston on January 9, 1861, participated in the capture of Fort Sumter on April 13, fought at the first battle of Cold Harbor in 1862, been wounded at Chancellorsville in 1863, and by 1864 was a first sergeant in a battalion of sharpshooters of McGowan's South Carolina brigade in the Wilderness campaign.

On May 16, 1864, he was taken prisoner behind Federal lines in the vicinity of Spottsylvania while posing as a Union scout. On May 23 he was shipped into the military prison at Point Lookout, Maryland, located where the Potomac empties into Chesapeake Bay. It was a bleak spit of white sand with whitewashed barracks where a glaring sun left the Confederate prisoners half-cooked and half-blinded. Two nights later, on May 24, Benson slipped into the bay and swam and waded his way to freedom. He was recaptured on May 31 while wandering near Mount Vernon. By June 5 he had been shipped to the Old Capitol Prison in Washington where he was put in a cell on the first floor.

Benson immediately began to chop through the floor of his cell in an attempt to reach the cellar from which he could escape. He was caught and moved to a cell on an upper floor. On July 24 he was removed from his cell and put aboard a prison train bound for Elmira, where he arrived the next day.

The first thing he did was to begin searching for a way to escape again.

The western end of the pond, which did not quite reach the stockade wall, interested Benson. He had

143

already made one escape by water from Point Lookout. Why not try another?

A 30-yard stretch of sandy soil between the end of the pond and the fence was in comparative darkness at night. Benson figured he could slip into the pond a short distance from his barracks, and then swin under cover of darkness down to the end near the fence. When the sentry was at the farthest point away on his post, Benson would crawl the 30 yards to the fence. In the darkness he would scoop a hole in the sand under it and escape.

The following night he slipped out of his barracks and saw the night was clear, the moon full. An attempt would have been foolhardy. He decided to wait for a night when the sky was cloudy.

The next night it appeared that the prison authorities had read Benson's thoughts. Huge railroad lights were mounted all around the perimeter of the camp inside the fence. From that night on the area was as brightly illuminated as a downtown city street.

Foiled by the railroad lights, Benson looked to the other side of the pond where it entered the prison under the fence, as an offshoot of the Chemung River. It was impossible for him to tell if the fence stopped just below the water line or had been pushed deep below the surface of the water, perhaps right to the bottom of the pond.

In any event, Benson figured that if he could reach the fence where it crossed the pond—without being spotted by the guards—he could get through. If the fence did not go to the bottom of the pond, he could dive under the boards and get out that way. If the fence went all the way to the bottom, he could cut a hole through it under water.

The trick was to reach the fence. He would have to weight himself down with rocks and stones in his pockets and then walk the fifty yards on the bottom of the pond. But how was he to breathe while under water?

As ingenious as he was tenacious, Benson fashioned a breathing tube from scraps of wood which he planned to insert in his mouth, keeping the other end above water as he walked along the bottom of the pond.

Before he tried to use it, however, he ran into two Georgia boys, prisoners like himself, with whom he'd gone to school before the war—John Perrin and Jim Bohler.

They invited Benson back to their barracks, a building in the northeast end of camp. There were 80 to 100 feet of bare ground from the back of the barracks to the nearest fence. On one side of their barracks stood a wooden building about four feet away. On the other side, some distance away, was another barracks.

Bohler nodded at the bare ground between their barracks and the fence. "There's a rumor," he said, "the Federals is going to put up tents there and move in more prisoners."

"I don't want to be around to see it when it comes," Benson said.

Perrin pointed at the building that stood off by itself.

145

"They're using that for a hospital right now. Makes it convenient for us if we get the chilblains."

Benson was only half-listening. His attention was focused on the four feet of space between his friends' barracks and the next building. There were no windows in either barracks overlooking that space, and the alley it made was boarded up at both ends. A man could stand inside that alley, Benson realized, and nobody would know he was there.

"Let's go inside," Benson said, "and you can show me where your bunks are."

Bohler and Perrin led Benson inside the barracks. As he had hoped, their bunk beds, one on top of the other, were situated against the wall that closed in the alley between their barracks and the next one.

"This is just right," Benson said. "The alley next door is a blind one, and we can reach it from here. We can go into that alley and start a tunnel in the space under the building next door, and nobody, not the guards or any of the other prisoners, would be able to see us. We could dig straight for the fence, eighty to a hundred feet away, and nobody would disturb us." The more Benson thought about his plan, the better it seemed—much more foolproof than his plan to walk underwater in Foster's Pond.

Bohler scratched his head doubtfully. "But how will we get into the alley?" he asked. "If we climb over, down at one of the ends where it's boarded up, the guards will see us and be suspicious."

"Here's what you do," Benson said. "Cut a square in the wall right behind your bunk where it'll be hard to

146

see. Like a trapdoor or a window. We can scrounge two strips of leather somewhere to make hinges. If anybody sees the trap door and asks you about it, tell them you cut it there so you can spit outside without getting out of your bunk. Tell them you have a bad cough or that you chew tobacco or something like that."

"Sounds like it might work," Bohler said.

"We can go through the trap door at night," Benson said, "out into the alley and under the building next door and start digging and nobody will see us, least of all the guards."

Perrin and Bohler agreed to the tunnel venture. The trap door was cut in the wall of the barracks and hinges made. Each night Benson and his two old schoolchums slipped throught the trap-door opening out into the alley and under the building next door where they began to dig in complete secrecy. They went down on their knees and scooped out a hole in the ground, getting rid of the dirt by piling it up in a corner of the crawl space.

The three novice diggers soon realized they had their work cut out for them, and that digging a tunnel 80 to 100 feet long was no easy job. After discussing the risks involved, they took in three more diggers to spread the work around.

A few days after the newcomers joined Benson's tunnel group, one of them approached him and said that he would like to speak to him privately. The two men walked a short distance from the barracks and squatted in the sun.

"Sergeant Benson," the man said, "not only am I

digging a tunnel with you, but I'm working on another tunnel in the camp with some other men. The man in charge of that tunnel is Sergeant Joe Womack. He has some business he'd like to talk to you about."

"What kind of business?"

"Maybe the sergeant better tell you that himself."

"All right," Benson said. "Let's go."

Benson accompanied the digger to a barracks near the center of the compound. Since the Federal authorities were short-handed, a Confederate prisoner had been put in charge of this barracks. He was a cavalry sergeant-major, a big man, his face darkly tanned from life in the field. Unlike many of the prisoners, who went barefoot, he wore shoes of good quality. Sgt. Joe Womack was obviously a man who knew how to take care of himself.

"Sergeant," Womack said, "I understand you're digging a tunnel."

"That's right, Sergeant," Benson said, "and I hear you are doing the same."

"Right. And I'm going to suggest that you give up *your* tunnel."

"*What?*"

Womack tried to reassure Benson. The more tunnels being dug, he said, the better the chance the prison authorities would stumble on one of them. Once that happened, they'd start a careful search, and all other tunnel operations would be endangered.

"Our tunnel is going to be a much shorter one than yours," Womack said. "We're bound to go under the fence first and go out. And when we do, the Yankees will start looking and find yours. All your tunnel can mean is trouble. Simply because it exists, it's a danger to ours. If it's discovered before ours is finished, all it will have done is put us out of business."

"Where does that leave us if we quit?" Benson asked.

"Just close your tunnel down and come in with us."

"Where is your tunnel?"

"Will you give me your word you will come in with us?"

"Yes," Benson said, "if what you say is so."

"We're digging under Hospital No. 1," Womack said.

Benson whistled softly in admiration of Womack's choice of a starting point for his tunnel. Hospital No. 1 was the first and northernmost building in a line of six at the west end of the camp, just inside the road from the Dead-House. It was a short 16 feet from Hospital No. 1 to the fence.

Benson's diggers needed no convincing when he returned and said they had been invited to join a group that had a 16-foot tunnel under way. The shorter the tunnel, the better.

III

Benson and his diggers closed up their tunnel and sealed the trap door in the barracks wall. That night they crawled under Hospital No. 1 and began taking their turns at digging in Womack's tunnel.

For the next three nights the digging continued. On the fourth night, when the tunnel had been pushed eight feet, the diggers assembled at the mouth—only to discover that somebody had been there before them and filled it up with dirt.

Shocked and unable to understand what had happened or why, they did no digging that night, but dispersed to their barracks. Womack and Benson held a conference.

"Who could have done it?" Womack asked.

"Let's think this thing through," Benson said, "and figure all the possibilities. Surely the Yankee guards didn't do it. If they'd found our tunnel, they wouldn't waste time shoveling dirt into it. They'd let us keep on digging until we were almost under the fence and then they'd break our tunnel open and throw us all in the jail. And you and me in the sweat-box because we're non-coms."

Womack bit off a plug of tobacco and chewed thoughtfully for a few minutes. "You know what I'm thinking?" he said finally.

"The same thing I am," Benson said. "That some of our own men in camp did it. That they got a tunnel working near us and we missed it. They were afraid we'd finish first—and when we made the break, their tunnel would be discovered."

"But where is it?"

"Tomorrow night," Benson said, "we take a look. And my bet is that it's right next door—under Hospital No. 2."

The following night Benson and Womack stretched out on the ground under Hospital No. 1 on its south side, facing Hospital No. 2, while the other members of their group set about cleaning out their tunnel. Soon they saw many men slip through the shadows and under Hospital No. 2.

"That explains it," Benson said. "Now we know who sabotaged our tunnel."

"What we going to do about it?" Womack asked.

"Join them," Benson said. "It doesn't make any difference which tunnel we escape through. I'll take a couple of our boys and go over and dig with them. Whichever tunnel finishes first, we go through it."

Benson and some of the diggers from the Hospital No. 1 tunnel moved over to the Hospital No. 2 tunnel. Nobody there questioned their right to join the group. It was a confused operation with too many men involved and no one in charge.

Strangely enough, the Yankee police sergeants who constantly prowled the camp day and night, missed the disorganized Rebel activity under Hospital No. 2. Instead, as luck would have it, their attention was drawn to the neat, efficient digging operation which had been resumed under Hospital No. 1.

One night Benson lay under Hospital No. 2 in the overcrowded disorganized bustle there, his heart sinking at thought of the noise and confusion. He was staring at the quiet darkness under Hospital No. 1 where his friends were industriously working away. He knew they were making good progress and either had

151

reached the fence or already passed under it. That night they planned to dig upward and make a small observation hole at the surface to check their position. If they had gauged themselves correctly and were beyond the fence, a breakout would surely follow the next night.

Lying a few feet from Benson and also looking toward Hospital No. 1 was a Rebel digger Benson did not know by name. He had not even had a good look at the man's face. Benson's attention had been drawn to the man because he appeared to be an odd sort. He was tall, lean, almost hawklike in appearance. He was barefoot and wore a long denim frock coat with tails that parted behind. Even more strange was the extremely long nail on the small finger of his left hand. What purpose could this long fingernail have?

Suddenly, from outside the fence, a rifle fired. Men yelled and there was the sound of a scuffle. Then, in unmistakable Yankee accents, came the cry: "I got him! He tried to duck back down the tunnel to warn the others, but I got him! Get over to the hospital and get the others before they get away!"

The sound of the guards running pell-mell reached Benson and the other men under Hospital No. 2. The Yankees could be heard scrambling over the fence wall and dropping inside the prison.

"The Yankees knew about the tunnel all the time," Benson said. "They were waiting for our boys to come up outside the fence!"

There was panic among the Rebels crowded under

Hospital No. 2. "Let's get out of here!" somebody cried.

The strange-looking Rebel near Benson turned and hissed into the darkness. "Silence back there! Don't anybody move or make a sound. The Yankees are after our boys in the other tunnel. They don't know we're here!"

As Benson watched, the darkness under Hospital No. 1 exploded into a mass of scrambling, frantically running Rebels. They fanned out quickly, heading in all directions, desperately trying to reach their barracks and tents before the Yankees were on them.

Yankee guards threw themselves into the darkness under Hospital No. 1, poking their bayonet-tipped rifles ahead of them. But it seemed that most, if not all, of the Rebels had already escaped, warned off by the rifle shot and the shouting when the first man had been taken as he poked his head out of the hole in the ground.

As Benson watched, two Yankee guards marched a Rebel prisoner away. It was the digger who had been captured.

"It was him, all right," said the man next to Benson. "That was J. W. Crawford they nabbed. He's for the prison jail sure enough."

The digging effort continued under Hospital No. 2. Finally the night came when the men planned to finish the tunnel and break through to the surface.

When Benson arrived at Hospital No. 2 that night, scores of men lounged in the area around the hospital buildings, whispering about the tunnel and its chances

153

of completion. He knew the situation was dangerous, like a bomb with a burning fuse. There was a slim chance that a few men might be able to make an escape, but it hardly seemed possible that so many could escape from the camp without the Yankees getting wind of what was going on.

Benson had lain under the hospital for about an hour when there was a sudden cry of alarm. "The Yankees are here!" somebody yelled. The cry passed from man to man, and the mass of humanity crammed under the hospital building stirred like a frightened animal. The first man who panicked took the rest with him. There was a wild scramble to get out.

Benson beat a hasty retreat with the others, then came to his senses. He saw no Federal guards. Walking back to the hospital, he crawled under the building. A few others came back, and the one man resumed digging.

When the digger in the tunnel came out, Benson removed his shoes and took his place. He chopped away at the hard-packed dirt with his knife until exhausted, then came out for air. He was lying near the mouth of the tunnel when a digger poked his head out and spoke to the man kneeling over the opening.

"I opened a small hole at the end of the tunnel," the digger said. "We've misjudged somehow. The hole is just inside the fence."

"*Inside?*" the kneeling man said incredulously.

"That's right. Inside. Pull a piece of sod and give it to me. I'll plug up the hole."

In the darkness neither man took notice of Benson

lying nearby. They conversed in low tones. "If the Yankees don't find it," the digger said, "we'll go out tomorrow night. If they find it—well—I'm in on another tunnel that was started a long time before this one was. You can come in with me on that one. I'll see you tomorrow night—and then we'll know what to do."

The other man was silent for a moment. "We've never seen each other," he said finally. "We've only met here in the dark to work on the tunnel. I'm not even sure what your face looks like. How will I know who you are so I can be certain I've got the right man and I'll be able to get in on your tunnel?"

The digger moved closer to the other man. "Here," he said, "you'll know me by this." He did something in the dark, but Benson, from where he was lying, was not able to make out what it was.

Then the two men were gone.

Benson tried to figure the puzzle out. How had the digger identified himself? What signal had he given the other man—by which he would know him in the dark? That signal could be a link to another tunnel— if this one was lost.

There was not much time left to think about it. Dawn was approaching. Benson slipped out from under the hospital and returned to his barracks where he fell into a troubled sleep.

It was afternoon when Benson awoke. His barracks was deserted—an unusual event. Usually his bunkmates were lying about, patching their clothes, playing cards, writing letters, or just sleeping.

He went outside and asked a prisoner hurrying

past, "Where is everybody? Where are you going in such a hurry?"

"Where have you been?" the man replied. "Haven't you heard? The Yankees found a tunnel under Hospital No. 2 and they're breaking it up with pickaxes and shovels now. Everybody's there. I'm going over to take a look. You want to come along?"

Benson shook his head, walked back into his barracks, and threw himself down on his bunk. All his work, all his digging in the tunnels had been for nothing. But maybe things weren't as black as they seemed. There was still another tunnel in existence. And if he could figure out the signal passed between the two men last night. . .

Suddenly Benson sat up. The digger had identified himself by putting out his *left* hand and touching the other man with it. He *had to be* the man with the long fingernail on the small finger of his left hand. "You'll know me by this," he had said. It was the one distinguishing characteristic that differentiated this man from every other prisoner.

For three days Benson searched for the man, hanging around the mess halls as various barracks came in for meals, checking the black markets where food was sold. Finally, on the fourth day, he spotted him—long fingernail, frock coat with the tails that parted behind. The man was strolling through the camp in a southerly direction.

Benson trailed him to the pond. The man stopped at the water's edge, then squatted on his heels. As Benson watched, he put his hand into a pocket, drew out a rock, and tossed it quietly into the water. Each time he waited until the ripples had settled before taking out another rock and throwing it into the pool.

Quietly Benson slipped up behind the man and stood there for a few minutes. "You'd better be careful," he said at last.

The man froze. His head swiveled round and his dark eyes examined Benson with distrust.

"What do I have to be careful about?"

"You don't have to be afraid of me," Benson said. "But if some of these other men see you throwing rocks in the pond, they may be able to guess you're getting rid of stones from a tunnel. Any one of them could be an informer—or even a Yankee spy in prisoner's clothes."

The man thought for a moment. Then he said, "How do I know I can trust you?"

Benson told him how they had dug under Hospital No. 2 together without ever really getting a good look at each other.

The man threw the rest of his rocks into the pond and then stood up. "Walk with me a little way," he said, "and tell me what you want."

"I want in on your tunnel," Benson said. "I'm a good digger and a hard worker and you can move faster with me in your party."

"One thing in your favor," the man said, "is that you found out about our tunnel yourself. So there's no point in my trying to hide it from you. And as long as you know about it, we'd be protecting ourselves by having

157

you work on it. Then you'd have an interest in the tunnel and not be likely to talk to anybody else about it. But I'm only one man in this group, and I'm not one of the original diggers. I'm a Johnnie-come-lately like yourself. I'll have to speak to the others first and see if it's all right with them. If they say it is, then you're in."

"Sounds fair to me," Benson said.

"Meet me before dinner tonight at the same place down at the pond where I was getting rid of the rocks. I'll have an answer for you then."

The two shook hands. Benson watched the stranger walk off, the tails of his coat flapping against his long lean legs. Although he did not know it yet, the odd-looking prisoner was named Washington Traweek and he had been a prisoner at Point Lookout in Maryland at the same time as Benson. Traweek, too, had attempted to escape from that camp by swimming out to sea. Where Benson had made it, Traweek had failed. He had succeeded in going through the surf undetected by the sentinels on shore and getting a quarter mile past the gunboats that were standing off the camp when he was seen and driven back to shore. Traweek was known to his fellow prisoners as a man with an indomitable fighting spirit, a tireless worker who never failed to deliver what he said he would do.

Benson was waiting at their meeting place on the shore of the pond when Traweek arrived late that afternoon. "They said you could come in," Traweek said. "They figured the same way I did. If you were smart enough to guess about the tunnel, they gain nothing by keeping you out. Maybe you can help us."

"I'll do my best," Benson said. "Nobody wants to get out of Elmira any more than I do."

"There's one thing," Traweek said. "You'll have to swear an oath not to betray our tunnel to any one. Is that agreeable to you?"

Benson nodded.

"Tomorrow morning," Traweek said, "you come at eleven o'clock to the tent in the northeast section of camp that is the third from the east end in the second row of tents from the fence. We'll be waiting for you."

"I'll be there," Benson said.

The following morning, at the appointed hour, Benson arrived at the tent. Traweek was waiting for him with several members of the digging party. They had all heard Traweek's account of how Benson had tracked him down, and they eyed him curiously.

Jack Scruggs, one of the "sick sergeants" who tended the ill prisoners in the tents, handed Benson a Bible. The men, including Benson, kneeled. John Fox Maull, a heavy-set six-footer who had been in Carter's Battalion of the Jeff Davis Artillery, was the man who had conceived and started this tunnel. It was he who administered the oath of secrecy to Benson. Ten minutes after Benson had taken the oath, he had turned his shirt and trousers inside out and was down digging in the tunnel.

The tunnel had already been pushed 12 feet in the direction of the fence when Benson joined the group. "How many feet do we have to go to reach the fence?" Benson asked when he emerged from his first digging session.

159

"Fifty-six feet more," grinned John Putegnat, a 19-year-old cavalryman. "We measured it *exact*—right under their Yankee noses."

"How'd you do that?"

"We was pitching rocks at the fence," Putegnat said, "right from outside the tent. There was a Yankee guard no more than 10 feet from the fence inside the camp. After a while he got tired of watching us. So I tied a thread to one of the rocks and threw it at the fence. The rock hit the fence and dropped dead. We pulled the thread back slow each time the guard turned his back. When we got it all in, we measured it. It ran 68 feet. That leaves us 56 feet of dirt and rock we still got to scrape our way through."

The opening of the tunnel was a shaft that went straight down into the earth inside the tent for four feet. It had been dug with a shovel stolen by one of the men while on a road detail. The tunnel leveled out then, and the men found they no longer could use the shovel. It was too big and clumsy, and they had to dig with a knife.

Getting rid of the rocks they dug out of the tunnel was a difficult problem. They had to be carried inside shirts, pants pockets, or coats, and then thrown into the sinks or the pond—anywhere they would not attract attention when they dried out and changed color.

One day there was a sudden, unexpected inspection of quarters, and the tunnel was almost exposed. Two men were digging in it when a Yankee officer and guards came down the line of tents. The diggers hurriedly planked over their hole and covered the planks with dirt and grass. One man feigned illness and lay down over the camouflaged opening—and the hasty arrangement passed the casual inspection. But after that the men took their orderly sergeant into the group—a man from South Carolina named Brawley—who did no digging but kept the others posted well in advance of any inspection. To keep casual passersby out of the tent one of the men was posted at the opening where he warned off strangers by saying a man inside was sick. Jack Scruggs, the "sick sergeant," who drew rations for the men ill in the tents, was able to get extra food for the diggers so that they could maintain their strength. He brought them two buckets of soup each day along with a few loaves of fresh bread.

Benson looked constantly for ways of improving the tunnel operation. One of the first changes he made had to do with the removal of freshly dug dirt. There was too much crawling just to get the debris back to the tunnel mouth. Benson worked out a system with a box which had two long cords attached to it. This was pulled back and forth from the digger to the mouth of the tunnel. He started the men chucking the stones under the wooden barracks buildings instead of tramping with them all the way to the pond. Next he realized that the rats which swarmed in the camp were a natural ally to the plot; he had the men begin dropping stones into their holes and warrens.

Work was progressing smoothly when—suddenly—disaster struck. Washington Traweek was picked up by the Yankee guards and led off to the prison commandant's office.

161

IV

At first the men thought their tunnel had been discovered and called operations to a halt. Then, when no raid materialized, they discarded that theory.

"The Yankees would have closed our tunnel down immediately—if they knew about it," Benson said, "not just drag Traweek off."

"Maybe," Putegnat suggested, "they're exchanging Wash for a Yankee in a Rebel jail. Or maybe he got a package from a friend in the north."

"We'd have heard about it if it was an exchange," Benson said. "It doesn't sound likely. And if it was something else, Traweek would be back with us now."

The mystery of where Traweek had been taken—and why—worried the diggers. They did not know whether to dig or go into hiding. And then Jack Scruggs, the "sick sergeant," came to the tent and told them what had happened to Wash.

Traweek had been marched to Major Colt's desk at camp headquarters. There Mott Conklin, the sergeant of the guard, ordered him to stand at attention while Major Colt came around his desk, looked Traweek over carefully, then felt inside his pockets and shoes for signs of fresh, moist tunnel dirt.

"You're one of the tunnelers," Colt stated flatly.

"I don't know what you're talking about, sir," Traweek replied.

"Then I'll explain," the Yankee major said. "This morning Sgt. Conklin did a final check of the tunnel he discovered under the Hospital No. 2 building before having a detail of men fill up the opening. He found a piece of paper in the tunnel—an order on the sutler for tobacco—with your name on it, W.B. Traweek."

The Major paced back and forth, pinching his jaw between long bony fingers. "I understand you men turn your clothes inside out when you dig in your tunnels in your foolish escape attempts. That's when you probably lost this paper." Major Colt picked up a dirt-encrusted form for drawing rations at the sutler's store from his desk. He held it where Traweek could see it, and see his own name plainly marked on it.

"Must be some kind of mistake," Traweek said. "I think I traded that paper away for some crackers to another prisoner a couple of weeks ago."

"Very unlikely," Major Colt said. "But we're not going to argue the issue. What I want from you are the names of the men who were digging that tunnel with you."

"I don't know what you're talking about, Major," Traweek said.

Major Colt smiled coldly. He crooked a finger at Sgt. Conklin. "Convince this prisoner, sergeant," he said, "that I mean business."

Conklin and two Yankee guards fitted a strait jacket around Traweek's chest and arms. Pressure was applied, the straps screwed down tighter and tighter until Traweek gasped with pain. After a minute or two of this treatment, he was released.

"What are the names of the prisoners who worked in the tunnel with you?" Colt asked.

"I'll see you in hell first, Major," Traweek replied.

At that moment a Yankee officer, Captain Bennett Munger, stepped forward. "Let me have this boy for a few minutes, Major," he said, "and I'm sure he'll tell me everything he knows."

Colt nodded permission, and Captain Munger led Traweek to a small room and closed the door behind them. He revealed he was a Yankee teacher who had taught school in Summerfield, Alabama, and remembered having had Traweek for a pupil. It was not a falsity to try to gain Traweek's confidence. Traweek remembered Munger.

"Make it easy on yourself, lad," Munger said, "and if you know them, give the Major the names he wants."

"I swear," Traweek said, "it was dark. I could not see their faces. I did not know the names of the men who were digging under the hospital."

Munger accepted Traweek's story and convinced Major Colt that the prisoner was telling the truth. Traweek was put in a cell with another man—Crawford, who had been captured the night the Yankees set the trap for the tunnel under Hospital No. 1.

That was almost the end of Jack Scruggs' story.

"What do we do now?" Maull asked. "Suppose we finish the tunnel. Do we leave Traweek behind in the camp jail after all the work he's done?"

"We'll break him out of the jail first," Benson said.

"Wait," Scruggs said. "There's a bit more. Traweek gave me this to give to you, Maull." He held a thick chunk of bread.

"What do I want this for?"

Scruggs grinned. "Break it open and you'll find out."

Maull tore the bread into two pieces. It came apart more easily than he expected and a piece of paper fluttered to the ground. Maull picked it up and read it. Then he looked at the others. "Traweek says that with a file he can fix it up so as to get out when the tunnel is ready."

None of the tunnelers had enough money to buy a file in the camp black market or to have one smuggled in. Late that afternoon, however, the portly Maull visited the section of camp where prisoners fashioned rings, bracelets, and other bits of jewelry for sale to other prisoners and Yankee guards. He was able to steal a small, hard file which he brought back to the tent and carefully inserted in Traweek's piece of bread.

Maull handed the chunk of bread to Scruggs. "Give this back to Traweek," he said. "Tell him I've lost my appetite."

Two mornings later a note came back to Maull from Traweek in his cell. "Everything is all right now," he wrote. "My bars are filed through. I am ready to come out when you finish the tunnel. Let me know one day in advance. Yrs truly, Wash."

The tunnelers settled down to steady digging. The tunnel was their master, the pivot around which everything else revolved.

One evening Benson came to the tent and found Traweek sitting on one of the bunks, grinning. With him was Crawford, his cell mate. Benson let out a yell of joy and slapped Traweek on the back.

"You didn't bust out of the camp jail, did you, Wash?"

"Nothing like that." Traweek chuckled. "Major Colt made me promise I wouldn't dig any more tunnels, and then he let us go out of the goodness of his black Yankee heart." Traweek nodded at his cell mate. "You know Crawford. He was in my cell. If you're agreeable, along with the other boys, I'd like him to take the oath and dig with us."

Crawford was sworn into the group, and the tunnelers went back to work. One thing that troubled them was just how far the tunnel had gone. Were they near the fence or not?

To settle the issue, Traweek went into the tunnel with one end of the thread they had used to measure the distance from their tent to the fence. When he returned, he said, "Strange! I went as far as the thread would let me go—and I still didn't reach the head of the tunnel. That should mean we've reached the fence and passed it."

Benson said, "If we'd reached the fence, we would have hit one of the fence posts already. If we'd gone under the fence, we would have heard the sentry marching on the platform right over our heads. Instead he sounds some distance away."

The tunnelers looked at one another. It was dawning on them that they didn't know exactly where they had dug to. For all they knew, Traweek remarked, "We could be coming up inside Major Colt's office, and then we all go into the jail house together."

Benson offered a suggestion to which the others agreed. After some difficulty he borrowed a ramrod from a prisoner who owned one. Traweek carried it to the head of the tunnel and thrust it a couple of inches above the ground. Then they saw they had reached a point about 18 feet from the fence.

They put a stone over the barely perceptible hole in the ground and went back to the tent where they talked the situation over.

"I don't see," Putegnat said, "how we managed to drift so far off course the way we did—and got over on the right instead of going in a straight line."

"We're all right handed, aren't we?" Benson said.

The men looked at one another and nodded.

"That explains it then," Benson said. "When you get up at the head of the tunnel, you're cramped for space. So you lie on your left side, and dig with the knife in your right hand. That's what we've been doing. And without realizing it, we've been digging in a long curve to the right."

"That sounds reasonable," Traweek said, "but it doesn't get us any closer to the fence. How do we make sure now that we're going in a straight line and not around in circles? We want to hit that fence in the smallest amount of time by the shortest route possible. But how?"

The solution, it appeared, would be in finding a way of signaling to a man in the tunnel from above ground without attracting the attention of the guards. Someone finally suggested a stick, with notches cut in its ends, top and bottom, running in the same direction. This was made, and a man in the tunnel ran the stick up through the ramrod hole. The men above ground turned the stick until the notch on the top of the stick pointed on a straight line for the fence. The notch on the bottom of the stick, inside the tunnel shaft, pointed at the fence too. Then the man in the tunnel marked the new direction and started digging.

In order to get fresh air to the digger, the ramrod hole was widened to a diameter of about three fingers. The hole was covered with stones during the day and uncovered at night. At that point the tunnel was dug out left and right on both sides to make a chamber underground. This the men called their "ventilator." It was about big enough for a man to sit in, hunched over, his knees drawn up to his chin.

As the cylinder of earth that had to be chopped through before the fence was reached grew shorter and shorter, the pace of digging became more intense. Finally, the last few yards were assaulted in a steady marathon of digging by the two strongest workers, Wash Traweek and Berry Benson.

Both pushed the tunnel hard, beyond the point of normal endurance. Finally, they grew careless. Traweek, who was digging, cried out hoarsely, "Benson, I've got to have air. Start backing down the tunnel."

"Wait," Benson called.

Traweek coughed. "What is it? Quick, I can't breathe."

"Let's make the change in the ventilator chamber instead of crawling all the way down the tunnel."

168

"It'll never work," Traweek said. "There isn't enough room. Start moving."

"I'm flat against the wall of the ventilator. Come on."

Traweek could not argue longer. Gasping for air, he pushed himself back down the tunnel, feet first.

Traweek reached the ventilator chamber. Benson felt Traweek's feet scrape past his face. Then Traweek's knees and legs moved past his head. They started the shift, Benson moving forward as Traweek scraped past him.

The two men were even with each other, face to face, each pressing his back as hard as he could against the wall of the chamber, trying to move in opposite directions, when they got stuck. Jammed together in the darkness, they could not move an inch. They had plugged up the tunnel with their own bodies as effectively as if they had filled it with rocks, earth, and concrete.

"We're wedged in," Traweek groaned. "It's no use."

"Try," Benson urged. "Try."

They strained—and locked themselves in tighter.

"Try again," Benson cried.

The two men lurched. There was the sound of clothes tearing and buttons ripping loose and suddenly Benson was free and moving past Traweek.

The pressure they had put on the unshored-up walls was too much of a strain. As Benson broke free, he took some of the tunnel with him. The roof and part of the wall collapsed and dirt and stone rained down. It filled Benson's eyes, nose, and mouth, and he retched violently, his body convulsing. Dirt covered his legs and feet. The tunnel was plugged behind him. He called to Traweek, but there was no answer.

Benson forced himself to lie quietly to conserve his strength and air. A minute or two passed and then he felt a movement about his feet. It was Traweek's hand, scraping away at the dirt.

"You all right, Benson?"

"I'm alive."

"I'll have the dirt out of here in a couple of minutes."

Benson forced himself to wait patiently as Traweek scooped the dirt out a handful at a time, filled the box, and sent it back to the mouth of the tunnel. The box traveled back and forth several times. Finally the tunnel was clear again.

"Do you want to come out and rest for a while?" Traweek asked.

"No. As long as we made the change, and almost killed ourselves in the process, I'll go forward and dig."

"All right," Traweek said.

He waited until he heard Benson crawl forward to the head of the tunnel and then started back to the ventilator. As soon as Traweek reached the chamber, he started hacking chunks of earth out of its walls, enlarging it. After Traweek was finished, he and Benson were able to change places in the ventilator chamber with no trouble. After that, when the digger became tired and needed fresh air, he merely had to go back to the ventilator instead of crawling backwards to the mouth of the tunnel, and the digging was speeded up considerably.

Early in the predawn hours of October 6, 1864,

Traweek was digging in the tunnel when his knife struck something hard with a dull, wooden sound. There was no question in his mind as to what he had hit. He pushed himself a few feet back down the tunnel and called out to Benson.

"I've hit a fence post," he cried.

"Change places with me," Benson said. "I want to take a look."

Traweek backed down the shaft to the ventilator chamber. The exchange was made, and Benson crawled forward to the head of the tunnel. He put his hands out and fumbled with the dirt in front of him, his fingers searching the wall. Then he felt it, a different texture from the earth and rocks, something round and splintery. He worked around it with his knife, cleaning away the dirt and rocks until the object was revealed for what it was without any doubt—the rough, irregular, rounded surface of a wooden shaft.

They had reached the fence.

Benson lay there for a few moments, every muscle and bone in his body aching, physically exhausted, savoring the moment, a feeling of rapture sweeping over him, dulling the pain. And as he lay there, the silence was broken by a steady thumping sound. At first he thought it was the sound of his own heart beat. But the sound became louder as it approached him. For a moment, the thump-thump sound was at its loudest and seemed to be in the tunnel with him. Then it began to recede. And Benson realized he had heard the footsteps of the guard overhead as he paced his beat on the elevated platform.

171

The two backed down the tunnel and told the news to the others. It was decided to wait through the day, then punch through the final few feet of the tunnel when the night fell. They would get out of the camp around midnight. Once outside, they planned a rendezvous at a barn they could see north of the prison.

They drew lots to determine the order in which they would go out. Traweek won the draw and was slated to be first. Crawford was second, Maull third. The others, Scruggs, Malone, Putegnat, and so on, would follow in that order. Benson was next to the last on the list, but it did not trouble him.

The morning of October 6 he walked from the tent into bright sunlight. Strolling to his barracks, he assembled his escape equipment: two pocket knives, half of a mess kit to be used as a cooking utensil, a pocket compass, and some strong cord from which he planned to fashion a bridle if he were able to steal a horse when he got out. The compass had been bought for 30 cents in the camp black market.

Benson had no intention of abandoning good friends with whom he had planned other escape attempts: John Perrin, Jim Bohler, Sgt. Joe Womack, Jack Kibler, two sergeants named Wilder and Johnson. He was honor bound not to tell them of the tunnel and the impending escape because of the oath he had sworn. But he was determined to take these men with him when he left the camp through the tunnel. And he intended to do this by stepping aside when it came his turn to enter the tunnel. He would let the last of the ten tunnel diggers go out ahead of him. When he was alone and the last man had left, he intended to awaken his friends and lead them out through the tunnel. He would have kept the terms of the oath he had sworn—and he would have paid off all debts to the men who had befriended him in camp.

That night, October 6, 1864, the tunneling party assembled in Maull's tent. Benson went into the tunnel first and Traweek followed him. Benson would finish the digging job and Traweek would send the dirt Benson dug out back down the tunnel in the box. The dirt would then be dumped inside the tent that last night instead of being distributed around the camp.

Benson hacked away at the earth wall in front of him with his knife, but it was slow going. It took him about two hours to go a yard and a half—just enough so that he got past the fence and was sure he was outside the prison. He certainly didn't want to come up in the middle of West Water Street. When he figured he was beyond the platform on which the sentries paced their rounds—where the tunnel opening would come out concealed in the shadows—he started to dig upwards.

The first few inches were still compacted earth. Then it changed to a pebbled texture. Benson put his knife aside and began to gouge out the earth with his fingers. Small stones and dirt fell on him. Finally his hand broke through to the surface and a stream of cold, fresh night air blew down on him and into the tunnel.

"Traweek," he called in a whisper, "come up and get some air!"

"You've broken through!"

"I sure have. Come here and get some clean air in your lungs."

The two men changed places. Traweek stayed but a moment at the end of the tunnel and then came back to the ventilator. Benson went forward to finish the job. He carefully gouged out the earth around the small hole he had made, leaving a thin shell a few inches thick between himself and the surface. This shell would be easy to break through for the first man who went all the way through the tunnel to the outside, and yet concealed the existence of the tunnel from on ground level. His shell completed, he dug a hole straight down in the bottom of the end of the tunnel so that, in a little while, when they broke through the shell to the surface, the earth would have a pit to fall into and not plug up the end of the tunnel. Then he and Traweek backed down the tunnel to the tent.

The tunnel, 68 feet long, a cylindrical shaft just wide enough in diameter to permit the passage of a man stretched out, sliding along 4 feet below the surface of the earth, was finished. It had taken from 9 o'clock on the night of August 24 to a little after midnight on October 7.

Back in the tent the men got ready to go. Each man assembled the small pile of equipment he would carry with him on his journey south through the enemy territory and stuffed it in his pockets.

A few minutes before 3:30 A.M. on October 7, Traweek stood up and patted his pockets. "All right, Crawford," he said, "it's time we got moving. Let's go."

Traweek went first into the tunnel. He would go the length of the shaft, break the crust, and emerge outside the prison—if all went well. Crawford went into the tunnel second, and Maull followed him shortly after.

Benson was exhausted from the digging. He knew it would take Traweek quite a while to crawl down the tunnel, break through the crust to the surface, and then make certain it was safe to emerge outside the prison. Crawford and the heavy-set Maull would use up precious time, too. There didn't seem to be any point in sitting around and waiting anxiously for his turn to come. He might as well get some rest. Asking the man ahead of him in the exit order to wake him before he went into the tunnel, Benson rolled up his coat and used it as a pillow. In a few minutes he had dozed off and was asleep.

Some time in the early hours of the morning Benson awakened. There were still three men besides himself in the tent; they were arguing excitedly, a note of panic in their voices.

"What's happening?" Benson asked.

Shelton, one of the men who had never done any digging and whose sole contribution had been in getting rid of dirt and rocks, turned to Benson. "The first six men are still in the tunnel," he said. "They're struck there."

"That's not possible, Benson said. "They'd suffocate in the tunnel. There's not enough air in there for six men."

"I tell you it's true," Shelton said. "I heard them. Go

in and see for yourself, if you don't believe me. If I'm wrong, yell back to us, and we'll follow you out."

"Yes," one of the other men pleaded, "you go in ahead of us, Benson."

As soon as he heard that, Benson knew that the nondiggers had panicked. They were afraid to go into the tunnel, and there was nothing he could do about it. The black hole in the earth, into which they had to commit themselves on faith if they wanted to escape, had paralyzed their minds and wills. He might be able to get them moving, and he might not.

"All right," Benson said, "I'll go first." It was disheartening to say it. It meant he could not remain behind to take his friends out with him. But he had no choice. If he wanted to get out at all, he had to enter the tunnel now.

Benson let himself down into the hole in the floor of the tent and then crawled forward into the tunnel. He knew every bump in the floor and the ceiling by now, and he moved forward rapidly. By the time he had reached the ventilator chamber he could feel the cool air blowing into the tunnel from the opening at the end. He knew then, as he had suspected before entering for this journey, that the tunnel ahead of him was empty and that the first six men had gone all the way through.

He called back down the tunnel to Shelton to tell him that there was nobody in the tunnel, and then went on. He took the left turn after the ventilator where they had corrected and followed the angle towards the fence. In a few moments he could see the glow of the night sky coming down the tunnel opening where Traweek had broken through to the surface. He scrambled the last few feet to the end of the tunnel. The fresh night air smelled sweet to him.

V

Benson raised himself cautiously, wriggling his head and shoulders out of the hole. He was in the shadows of the elevated sentry walk that ran around the top of the fence. Directly across the street from him was the observation tower, 30 to 40 feet from base to platform. Federal guards on the platform could look over the fence and across the camp. A few feet from the base of the observation tower three Yankee guards crouched around a fire, warming their hands against the night chill.

Benson boosted himself all the way out of the hole and then crawled to his right, away from the guards and toward the northeast corner of the camp. There he stood up and waited for a few minutes in the shadow of the sentry platform, working up the courage to make his break and walk out into the open, away from the camp.

Forcing himself not to break into a run, he stepped out. He crossed the street, expecting a bullet in the back at any moment. But nothing happened. He reached the other side of the street and started walking east.

Before he came to the end of the block, he vaulted over a sidewalk fence into a front yard. Suddenly, a dog rushed him. He raced for the fence behind the house and scrambled over it just ahead of the dog's snapping jaws. Finding himself in a lane, he started running. He kept on, working his way north and east to the edge of Elmira where he began to climb a high hill the prisoners had been able to see from inside the camp.

Part way up it, he looked back at the camp. The railroad lights, mounted on the fences, made the prison a glaring patch in the fading darkness of early morning. The sentries, diminished by distance, paced along the fence platform like toy soldiers. The tents were sheets of white, the barracks black oblong spots. The camp slept. All was quiet. The escape had not yet been discovered.

Benson tore himself away from the sight, turned his back, and scrambled on through the underbrush, up the hillside. Finally he reached the barn the tunnelers had set as their meeting place while they were still inside the camp. Approaching it cautiously, he whistled softly. There was no response.

"Traweek!" Silence greeted him. "Maull! Putegnat! Scruggs!"

All was quiet. Benson crawled forward and then slipped into the barn. No one was there. He was on his own.

As daylight grew, Benson plunged into a forest and pushed on as fast as he could go. As soon as he felt he was safely away from the immediate area of the camp, he headed due west.

Hiding and sleeping in empty schoolhouses, farm sheds, under churches, and in culverts when he was caught in the open at night, he traveled through the

unfamiliar countryside by day. He took his directions
from his compass, a rough penciled sketch map, and the
road signs and mileposts he encountered on his way. He
passed undetected through the village of Big Flats and
the town of Corning, then turned south, passing into
Pennsylvania near Lawrenceville. He lived off the
county, eating apples and nuts, drinking water from
streams, stealing and cooking an occasional chicken.
Eventually he covered his tattered uniform with bits of
civilian clothing he stole from clotheslines and through
open windows.

Sometimes boldly asking directions of Northerners
he met, claiming he was in search of a runaway horse,
Benson passed through Canton on October 11, 1864.
By October 13 he was in Williamsport. He left the town
by following the railroad tracks to the Susquehanna
River. Then he paralleled the river, walking the
railroad tracks until he became footsore. As night fell,
he stole a rowboat and oars and began a restful ride
downstream. Abandoning his boat as the sun came up,
he slipped ashore. By 7 A.M. on Friday, October 14, he
was in the railroad yard at Northumberland. There he
hid aboard a lumber train for what he hoped would be a
long ride south. But the train went only a few miles, and
then its engine was detached at Sunbury.

Although the ride had been a short one, Benson was
quick to see the advantages of railway travel. He could
move a hundred miles at a clip toward the Confederate
lines if only he could pick the right train and stay out of
Yankee hands.

At Sunbury Benson mixed with the crowd in the railway station. When an express pulled in and there was a rush of people to climb aboard, Benson went with the crowd. He stayed on the platform of a car, watching through the glass door as the conductor came down the car collecting fares.

Just before the conductor reached the door, Benson went down the steps of the car. Putting his left foot on the bottom step and holding on to the car rail with his left hand, he flattened himself against the side of the car.

After he heard both car doors slam shut and knew the conductor had passed, he pulled himself back and sat on the steps. When the train arrived in Harrisburg, he learned another train was leaving for Baltimore in an hour.

At 1 p. m. Benson was aboard the Baltimore-bound train. Again he went to the platform at the end of the car. As soon as he saw the conductor approaching he went down the steps, and flattened himself against the side of the car.

This time he had not been quick enough, however. He felt a tap on his shoulder and swung his head around.

"What are you doing out there?" the conductor asked angrily.

"I'm going to York."

"Where is your ticket?"

"I don't have any."

"Get inside."

180

Benson Leaped from the Train

The conductor hooked his fingers on Benson's arm and pulled him back into the car. He eyed his odd assortment of unmatched civilian clothes suspiciously.

"You're stealing a ride, aren't you?"

Benson knew he might be turned over to the police. He was still wearing his Confederate uniform under the civilian clothes he had stolen. Once in the hands of the police, his identity would be established quickly. And then it would be a quick trip back to Elmira and solitary confinement.

"I live in Harrisburg," Benson said. "I received a telegram my sister in York is dying. I didn't have money for the fare, and I wanted to see her one last time."

"You should have told me," the conductor said gruffly. "You might have knocked your brains out on a rock bank on the outside of the car."

"I'm sorry," Benson said.

"Go inside the car and take a seat. We'll be in York soon. You can ride until then."

Benson took a seat and dozed until York. When the train pulled into the station he was tempted to stay aboard and continue on southward. But he did not dare.

Benson struck out south from York on foot. By Sunday October 16 he was at Cockeysville, Maryland, within 15 miles of Baltimore. There he saw a cattle train loaded with beef for Grant's army pull into the railroad yard to take on water. Federal soldiers rode shotgun on the tops of the cars.

Figuring that a bold front was the best way of

Benson Watched the Yankee Bivouac

concealing the fact that he was an escaped prisoner, Benson started running as the train began to move and pulled himself up on the ladder of the last car. He climbed to the roof of the car, nodded to the Yankee guard, and sat down next to him.

"Where are you headed for?" the soldier asked.

"Baltimore."

"Live around here?"

"Yes. Out in the country a few miles from town."

"Were you here when the Rebels came?"

"I sure was." At the time he had been a prisoner in the Old Capitol Prison in Washington.

"What was it like?"

"When the Rebs were here. . . . ?" Benson mused. He looked out at the countryside. "See that bridge?" They burned that. Rode through that wheat field over there. Was so many of them they looked like ants."

"Must have been something," the Yankee guard said.

"Yes it was," said Benson.

At 11 A.M. Benson jumped from the train as it slowed to enter Baltimore. Brazenly he walked through the city streets, passing Sunday pedestrians on their way to church and police on patrol. He went to an address he had learned about in the prison camp. It was the home of a woman sympathetic to the Confederacy. But nobody had heard of her when he arrived there. All he could do now was to get out of the city as quickly as possible.

By dusk Benson was walking southwest out of Baltimore. He passed through Ellicott's Mills and then the town of Unity. His immediate goal was Leesburg, Virginia, where he hoped to obtain help at the home of Judge Gray, a Confederate sympathizer.

On the night of October 18 Benson crept up on a Yankee cavalry troop bivouacked at a crossroads. He watched the Yankee soldiers build cooking fires and make coffee, then skirted the encampment, slipped through the pickets standing guard, and continued on his way.

Late that night he heard the rushing waters of the Potomac River and knew he was close to the Virginia border. Leaving the road, he cut straight across the fields toward the sound of the river. On the way to the river he caught a grazing horse and bridled it with the cord he had brought from Elmira. The horse refused to take to the water, however, and after a long struggle Benson abandoned the animal and hid in the woods.

All day long on October 19 Benson lay in a small depression in the forest, covered with branches and twigs he had pulled over himself. The sounds of cannon fire came from the area of Winchester, some 20 or more miles away; although he did not know it, a battle was being fought by Sheridan's and Early's troops. The sounds of the firing drifted to the south in mid-afternoon, boding ill for the Rebel cause.

After night fell, Benson swam the Potomac. When his feet touched ground, he was in Virginia. But he still was in the border area of North and South, a region continually swept by troops and raiders of both sides.

Benson was put up for the night and fed by a

Confederate sympathizer near the river. Then he walked on to Leesburg and stayed there two days with Judge Gray. On Sunday evening, October 23, he blundered into a house where a detachment of Colonel John S. Mosby's Rebel raiders were encamped.

At first suspicious that Benson might be a Union spy, Mosby's men questioned him closely. They were tough men, and if he failed to pass their test he knew he would be hung.

"What's your regiment?" one asked him.

"1st South Carolina," Benson replied.

"Where is it now?"

"I don't know."

"Well, it's in Richmond," one of the Rebels said.

"What are you doing up here?"

"I was a prisoner of war. I escaped from Elmira."

The raiders studied him closely. They still weren't sure about him. They needed proof he was what he claimed to be. One left the circle of men around Benson and walked slowly to the fireplace. He poked at the embers with a short, razor-edged knife.

"They send you straight to Elmira from the front?" he asked.

"No," Benson said. "I was a couple of days at Point Lookout. I broke out of there but then I was retaken. I was in the Old Capitol for a while, and then I was sent north to Elmira."

"Who'd you see at the Old Capitol while you were there?" the man at the fire asked. "Any of Mosby's men, for instance?"

Benson tried to remember. He knew that the answer was crucial, that it might make a difference between his living—or dying at the hands of his own comrades. It would be an ironic end after he had escaped and come so far.

"I knew Ben Crowley and Sam Underwood," he said at last. "They were both Mosby men, and they were at the Old Capitol Prison the same time I was."

The tension in the room was relieved. The man at the fire sheathed his knife and grinned.

"He's all right, boys," he said. "Crowley and Underwood enjoyed the hospitality of the Old Capitol."

The interrogation was over. Benson heaved a sigh of relief. He was made welcome and Mosby's men insisted that he tell them all the details of his escapes.

The next morning Mosby's men saddled up to move out on a raid. Colonel Mosby himself had a few last words for Benson before they rode off.

"Stick to the Blue Ridge as you move south," he warned. "There are Federal patrols all over the area. You have to be careful when you come to the gaps or you may run into one of them."

Mosby and his men rode off and Benson continued on his journey south. On Thursday evening, October 27, he walked down a dusty country road into the arms of an advanced sentinel of General Bradley Johnson's cavalry. He had made contact with regular troops of the Confederate Army at last.

Benson was feted by General Johnson and his staff, then given a pass to New Market to report to General

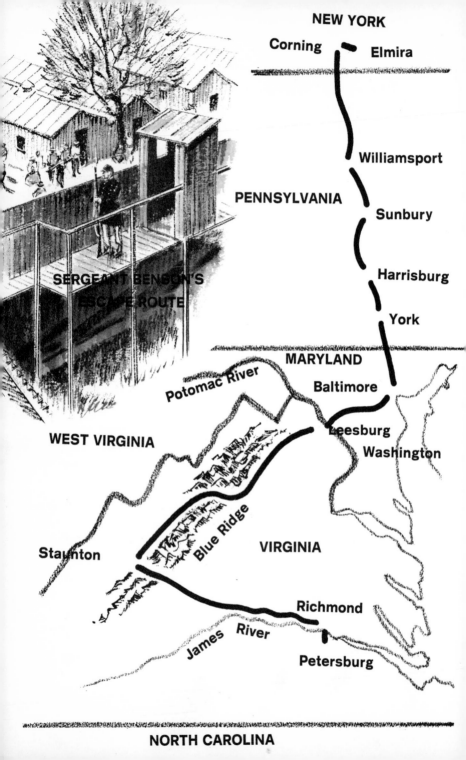

NEW YORK

Corning   Elmira

Williamsport

Sunbury

Harrisburg

York

PENNSYLVANIA

SERGEANT BENSON'S
ESCAPE ROUTE

MARYLAND

Potomac River

Baltimore

WEST VIRGINIA

Leesburg

Washington

Staunton

Blue Ridge

VIRGINIA

Richmond

James River

Petersburg

NORTH CAROLINA

Jubal Early. In New Market he ran into an old friend, Robert Hitt of the 12th Georgia Battalion, and learned for the first time that he long ago had been given up for dead by his family.

"They found a body on the beach at Point Lookout the day after you must have escaped," Hitt told Benson. "Michael Duffy of your regiment, who was exchanged later, thought it was you."

General Early gave Benson a pass to Richmond. He rode a stage coach to Staunton, then took a train to Richmond. There he sent a telegram to his father, saying he was alive and well and had just escaped.

Benson's regiment was south of Richmond in Petersburg. The train ride lasted an hour. In front of the Spottswood Hotel in Petersburg, Benson ran into one of his regiment's officers, who took him to his unit area. There, at the end of a company street, he saw his brother, Blackwood, facing the other way and cooking a meal over a fire.

As Benson went down the street, men recognized him and exclaimed in astonishment: *"There goes Sergeant Benson!"*

When he was within a few yards of his brother, a man cried: "Corporal Benson! Your brother's here!"

Blackwood Benson spun around. He was stunned when he saw the brother he had believed to be dead. But not for long. Running to him, he joyfully pounded him on the back.

Sergeant Berry Benson was home after digging his way through a tunnel 68 feet long and then traveling some 600 circuitous miles, much of it in enemy territory, in 20 days. He had averaged an incredible 30 miles a day.

Every one of the men who had gone through the tunnel with him also made the journey back to the Confederacy safely.

The day after he returned, Berry Benson was put on a scouting patrol with his brother, Blackwood, to seek out the enemy. Sergeant Benson had returned to the war.

ABOUT THE AUTHOR

A. I. Schutzer knows war at first hand. A U.S. infantry staff sergeant in Europe during World War II, he once spent two days making his way from behind the German lines after his outfit had been overrun. Schutzer holds the Bronze Star and Purple Heart. He has written widely on a variety of subjects for a great number of magazines. With his wife and daughter he lives in Tenafly, New Jersey.

Index